Stop Press

STOP PRESS

THE INSIDE STORY OF THE TIMES DISPUTE

ERIC JACOBS

ANDRE DEUTSCH

First published 1980 by
André Deutsch Limited
105 Great Russell Street, London WC1

Printed in Great Britain by
Willmer Brothers Limited
Rock Ferry, Merseyside

Jacobs, Eric
  Stop press.
  1. Times Newspapers Ltd dispute, Great
  Britain, 1978–1979
  I. Title
  331.89'281'072142   PN5124.S75

  ISBN 0–233–97286–2

*The author and publishers are grateful to
Times Newspapers for providing the photographs
between pages 70 and 71*

For Emma and Daniel

CONTENTS

PREFACE

This book had its origins in the instinct of the *Sunday Times*'s editor, Harold Evans, for a good story. When he suggested that I write it, in September 1978, there did not seem to be much to write about. All I knew was that Times Newspapers wanted to trim its staff and introduce some new methods, including electronic technology. Though the company had threatened to shut down if it did not get what it wanted, the sum of its ambitions appeared to be no greater than that of dozens of companies hard-pressed by labour disputes and other economic pains. Neither Evans nor anybody else guessed then that two great newspapers and their supplements would be silenced for almost a year in the longest labour wrangle involving a major employer in British memory. For if they had guessed, they would surely not have done what they did. I am indebted to Evans for his intuition that there was more in it than we knew, and also for the time in which to work on his idea.

Although Evans suggested it, this is not an official history. That will no doubt follow. Mine is a reporter's story, written from an unusually privileged position. After fifteen years writing about industrial disputes from the outside I now found myself, willy-nilly, on the inside. As an employee I shared the same anxieties about the dispute as all the others; as a very minor union negotiator I participated directly in some of the events; because I started keeping notes and records as soon as Evans proposed the book, I was well into the story even before there was one; and I knew most of the participants personally.

Though I am indebted to almost everybody named in the book for their help, I have decided to make no specific acknowledgements. Scholars live by disclosing their sources, but journalists are more used to discretion. It would be invidious to single out those who have been particularly helpful and, when events are so recent and issues still so sensitive, they probably would not thank me if I did.

Intimacy with people and events has great advantages for a writer, but it has perils too. To write about one's own colleagues is to become extraordinarily sensitive to the fine line that always separates fact from judgement. Few events in the dispute were unambiguous. If I talked to two people straight out of the same meeting, I got two different versions of what happened. Even written documents could be hard to decipher. What was I to make of a memo written by a director that I came across by chance while doing research for the book which said that I had applied for a job in management but that I was too foxy to be recommended? I had never actually heard of the job, let alone applied for it, until I read the memo. And as for being foxy, all I can say is that, when I challenged the author of the memo, he declared it was a compliment. Ho, hum. The significance of this incident eludes me still.

I have probably missed the point of other incidents too. For this I can only apologise. I have tried to concentrate on the most significant events in the evolution of the dispute, the things that made it what it was. This has meant leaving out other events. But to have tried to be comprehensive would have made the book intolerably long; and to have tried for total objectivity would have been impossible. One of the discoveries I made during the shutdown is that an industrial dispute is not an abstraction of numbers and masses but something that goes on, vividly and furiously, inside the heads and hearts of everybody caught up in it, my own included. I hope that other participants in the dispute will understand that there are limits to any one person's comprehension of what happened. But I also hope there are enough plain facts for readers to make up their own minds.

Eric Jacobs
August 1980

1
ANARCHY
AND
RUIN

When a compositor retires from a Fleet Street newspaper he is 'banged out'. Once all the pages for that night's first edition have been set in metal type and sent off to the foundry to be turned into plates, the companionship of men – the 'ship – with whom he has worked for many years seize hold of the tools of their trade and bang them together. For a minute or two a horrendous, echoing din reverberates around the great metallic workshop, a living marvel of Victorian mechanical ingenuity where the compositor's father and grandfather would have felt, and very likely did feel, entirely at home. The man – there are no woman compositors – stands, embarrassed, blinking back a tear. He has been 'banged out' once before, when he finished his apprenticeship, but now it is his farewell fanfare, his last parade. Afterwards there will be speeches, drinks, a presentation, then out into the utter darkness of retirement.

In the early evening of Saturday, 25 November 1978 a 'banging out' took place in the composing room of the *Sunday Times*. It was, perhaps, a little louder, a little longer, than usual. But nobody retired that night. It was no sentimental farewell to a colleague. The compositors were saying goodbye to their newspaper.

Times Newspapers had set a deadline for acceptance by its staff of sweeping changes in the way they worked. If the deadline was not met, then the company would close down all its five papers – the *Sunday Times*, the *Times*, the *Times Literary Supplement* and its two educational supplements – until they did. The deadline was now only five days away, and it was already obvious that it was not going to be met.

Standing at the bottom of the short flight of stairs which leads from the editorial floor down into the composing room, two senior managers, John Carr and George Banyard, listened, legs apart, arms folded, backs straight, unsmiling and unmoved. In the space between them and the compositors the *Sunday Times* editor, Harold Evans, hovered, a pen in one hand and a sheaf of galley proofs in the other. He did not quite know how to take it, whether to laugh or cry. Nor, it seemed, did the compositors themselves. Was this 'banging out' an act of defiance or just a joke between friends?

As the noise died away, George Darker, the head printer, murmured reassuringly to Evans: 'Never mind. They'll be doing it again next week.' But the composing room did not set type or make up the pages the next week, nor for many weeks and months after that, not until 17 November 1979, nearly a year later.

Those few moments seemed drenched in symbolism. They made a perfect vignette of industrial confrontation, in which management and union stared each other down in a rite of tribal defiance, while in the void between them the hapless newspaper, in the person of Harold Evans, hardly knew which way to turn, on which side its loyalties lay. Yet it was somehow good-humoured. Nobody lost his temper. There was no violence in the air or even much dislike – only a profound fatalism. It was as if everybody understood each other perfectly well but was trapped in his own role and his own loyalties and could not reach out across the void. Events must take their course; there was nothing anybody could do now.

Most poignantly symbolic of all were those very objects that produced the din of the 'banging out'. Chase, rule, galley, stone – venerable names of tools and methods of production that were centuries old and ingrained in the habits of mind of the craftsmen who used them and the union to which they belonged. Men and union, tools and workshop, they had grown to be of a piece with each other; but now the whole intricate structure of their relationship was at stake. Two floors below there waited a new and very different workshop, clean and carpeted, almost like an office in its quiet decorum, a feminine sort of place compared with the solid male muscularity of the old composing room. In the new workshop there would be no more 'banging out', for there was nothing to bang. There the clash and clank of the nineteenth century would give way to the hum and clicking of late twentieth-century electronic technology. Here in the composing room the changes the company sought were at their most tangible; elsewhere, in other departments of the newspaper, the changes were no less real.

I had no business to be there. Half an hour before I had helped to put the final editing touches to an article explaining why this was likely to be the last *Sunday Times* for a while, and in the ordinary way I would have gone back to my own room. But I had lingered in the composing room to read the proof of an article on the mass suicide in Guyana a week before of nearly a thousand followers of the cult leader Jim Jones. The parallel was irresistible, and I could not help making a note there and then : 'perhaps they felt the same ambiguity as they reached for their cyanide bottles.' Afterwards, in the Blue Lion pub on the other side of Gray's Inn Road, I laughed it off with a colleague, George Darby. The comparison was absurd. It was an abuse of the journalist's God-given right to mint his own wild clichés. But as the months went by it did not seem wild at all : it seemed chillingly accurate. We did not take it seriously because we had never heard of a mass industrial suicide. We were not to know how nearly it became just that, how slight, at times, was to be our newspaper's grip on life.

By the time of the November 'banging out' it was already almost seven months since we had first heard whispers that change was in the wind. On 10 April every member of the staff had been sent a warning letter by the chief executive of Times Newspapers, Marmaduke James Hussey, known to ally and enemy alike as 'Duke'.

The state of the newspapers which Hussey's letter described was one of anarchy and ruin. In the first three months of the year the company had lost £2 millions in revenue, drained away by a series of disputes which had frequently prevented completion of the night's print run of newspapers. The *Times* had failed to produce its full quota of copies on twenty-one occasions, the *Sunday Times* on nine and the *Times*'s supplements – the literary, education and higher education weeklies – on seven. 'No newspaper, even one as strong as the *Sunday Times*, can withstand such financial losses,' Hussey declared. 'Nor can we continue to put at risk the loyalty of our readers and the support of our advertisers.' All the disputes had been unofficial. If agreed procedures had been followed, there would have been no stoppages, no lost copies and no loss of revenue.

For months the whole of Fleet Street had been hit by the same wave of indiscipline, but Times Newspapers had suffered most. Hussey's letter only referred to the reason obliquely when it said the company would continue to observe the Labour Government's guidelines on pay, which had set an annual limit on wage rises of 10 per cent. What Hussey implied but did not spell out was that other national newspapers were ignoring the guidelines, leaving the pay of Times staff trailing behind the rest of Fleet Street.

Exactly what Fleet Street workers are being paid at any moment is obscure, even to the tax man. But there are good grounds for believing that Hussey was right. One measure of the rate of pay increases is reasonably accurate, if only because managements have no incentive to overstate it. That is the subscription that national newspapers pay to their own organisation, the Newspaper Publishers' Association (NPA), which is fixed as a proportion of the annual wage bill of each house. And the evidence from their subscriptions suggests that the typical Fleet Street newspaper paid its staff increases that were roughly twice as large as the Government wanted throughout Labour's three years of pay restrictions. When the Labour Government set a limit of 10 per cent, Fleet Street paid 20; and when the limit was 5 per cent, Fleet Street paid 10.

More direct confirmation of Hussey's hint is contained in a letter from one union leader to another, written in the summer of 1978. The letter reflected on the reasons for Times Newspapers' problems and came to one startlingly frank conclusion: 'Because this management have not made any under-the-counter deals in breach of Government pay policy,' it said,

> our members at the *Times*, over the last three years, have fallen from the top rung of the wages scale in Fleet Street to very nearly the bottom. There is no way that I or anyone else can persuade them this is just and fair, and we would be misleading management if we encouraged them to think this was possible. They have to find ways and means of restoring the position of our members if they are to return to the kind of relationship we all want.

But what 'ways and means' were open to the company? Paying up might be the easy way out, but it was also risky. No law enforced the pay limits, but the Government had warned that it would take what-ever action it could against any employer who breached its policy. One company had already lost its export credits, and the Thomson Organisation, to which Times Newspapers belongs, was peculiarly vulnerable to random Government revenge. The Organisation had one contract to fly British soldiers to and from Germany and another to publish the Yellow Pages telephone directories for the Post Office. It owned extremely profitable slices of the Piper and Claymore North Sea oilfields, which were closely regulated by Government, and its newspapers in London and the provinces carried a great deal of state advertising. Whether the Government would have denied the Organ-isation, say, a valuable flaring permit in the North Sea because Times Newspapers paid its staff too much must be open to doubt. But the board of the Organisation decided not to take the risk. It laid down that every one of its companies, including Times Newspapers, must hold strictly to the pay policy.

There was, however, a loophole in the policy. If a company could increase its efficiency so that it could pay more than 10 per cent with-out raising its prices, then it was free to go ahead. Without doubt, there was plenty of scope for that at Times Newspapers, as there was throughout Fleet Street.

In February, the *Times* lost four complete issues, and in March it lost five. The *Sunday Times* lost one issue in March and a second in April. This peak of wildcat stoppages brought things to a head. Gordon Brunton, the chief executive of the Thomson Organisation, summoned the executive board of Times Newspapers to his head-quarters in Stratford Place, off Oxford Street, and demanded action. The board was told to go away, think through its policy and return with firm proposals as soon as possible.

Brunton set the board an heroic task. It had to satisfy the Thomson Organisation, which wanted peace at the newspapers but not a peace bought at the expense of the Government's guidelines, and it had to satisfy the unions, which wanted far more money than the guidelines would allow. The only way to reconcile the conflict was through an efficiency deal. But inefficiency was ingrained in the Fleet Street way of life. Tackling it would mean dismantling dozens of ancient and easy-going practices and disrupting as many vested union interests in keeping them going.

How was Times Newspapers to achieve this trick? The board picked on a strategy which had been lurking at the back of its collective mind for years. It would present the unions with an ultimatum: either they accepted the company's plans for greater efficiency by a target date or the company would close the newspapers indefinitely and strike the staff off its payroll until the unions did accept. A shutdown – or the 'big bang' solution, as it came to be called – had been discussed as far back as 1971, when Hussey joined the company. Brunton himself had talked about it, even speculating the year before on November 1978 as a possible target date. Until now the company had fought shy of anything so drastic; Hussey in particular disliked the idea. Prolonged closure could ruin the newspapers; it might not persuade the unions; and in any case the company could not afford it. A desperate situation, however, called for desperate remedies – and the Organisation was richer than it had ever been.

Hussey returned to tell Brunton that the board had agreed to go for the shutdown strategy, but with one proviso. They wanted first to meet the print union leaders and to test the strategy out on them. Brunton agreed. He also offered to back up the shutdown threat by publicly issuing an instruction from the Organisation to Times Newspapers to go ahead with its plans. But Times directors did not like that idea. Far from strengthening their hand, they thought that an instruction would weaken it. Union leaders would see where true managerial power lay, and they would want to negotiate with the Organisation, not Times Newspapers, from the start.

Hussey contacted Bill Keys, general secretary of the Society of Graphical and Allied Trades (Sogat) and, as chairman of the print committee of the Trades Union Congress (TUC), effectively the doyen of trade unionism in the industry. Keys told him that his best chance of catching all the union leaders in the same place at the same time was in Birmingham, where they were due at a print industry conference. Hussey accordingly reserved two rooms at the Metropole Hotel, Birmingham, for 13 April.

The union leaders were a little taken aback when they saw the full panoply of directors Hussey brought with him for the meeting at the Metropole. Sir Denis Hamilton, the chairman and editor-in-chief, was not there. He had handed over executive responsibilities to Hussey several years before and was no longer a member of the executive board that ran the day-to-day business of the newspapers. But all the board members who were concerned with the newspapers were present, including Mike Mander, Hussey's deputy, primarily a marketing man who tended to avoid union matters, and the two editors, Harold Evans and William Rees-Mogg, of the *Sunday Times* and the *Times* respectively, who were even more inclined to stay in the background. The effect was calculated. Hussey wanted the union leaders to be in no doubt that the condition of the newspapers was very grave indeed.

Each director spoke up for his own sphere of interest. Dugal Nisbet-Smith, the general manager, went over the history of unofficial disputes and lost copies. Evans and Rees-Mogg underlined how the losses were damaging readers' confidence in the reputation and authority of their newspapers. And Mander spoke of his 'desperate concern' at the effect on advertising.

To at least one of the union leaders, Mander's presentation was the most persuasive. He quoted a letter from a director of Saatchi and Saatchi, the fast-rising advertising agency which was chosen to promote the Tory Party at the general election the following year. 'The service has now deteriorated to such an extent', the letter said, 'that there is very real danger of extra business being moved from your paper to other more reliable media.' According to Mander, there was 'the extremely frightening smell of a bandwagon beginning to move', set in motion by the disruption of Fleet Street in general and portending a switch of advertiser loyalty away from the national press. If just 2 per cent of advertising budgets were diverted from the newspapers, it would cost Fleet Street £34 millions in lost revenue. For Times Newspapers that would mean a drop in profitability of £4 millions, enough to move the company back into the red, from which it had only just managed to struggle clear.

When the directors had finished, Hussey turned to the union leaders. They now knew the nature and the scale of the problem: what was their answer? The question was directed to them collectively and individually – to Bill Keys, their chief spokesman; to John Jackson of the Society of Lithographic Artists, Designers, Engravers and Process Workers (Slade); to Ken Ashton of the National Union of Journalists (NUJ); to Owen O'Brien of the National Society of Operative Printers, Assistants and Media Personnel (Natsopa); and to Les Dixon of the National Graphical Association (NGA). All were general secretaries of their unions, the highest official each union had, except for Dixon, the NGA president, who was standing in for his general secretary, Joe Wade.

In the discussion that followed no clear, single solution was offered by the union leaders. But a common attitude emerged, or so it seemed to Hussey and his fellow directors. That attitude, as it came across the table to them, could be summed up as follows: we trade unionists agree with you that what is happening in Fleet Street is anarchic and has to be stopped; we think you are the company most likely to act decisively; if you do, we will support you; the very worst thing you could do is to start and then draw back; if you do that, we will wash our hands of your affairs. When the idea of a shutdown was put to the union leaders, they appeared to be strongly in favour, even to the point of encouraging the board to set a deadline for November there and then.

Their response was sufficiently encouraging for Hussey to arrange another meeting eleven days later at the Waldorf Hotel in London, this time without the editors. Before the second meeting Hussey sent Keys the draft of a letter containing the outlines of his strategy, and two days after the meeting he dispatched a revised version of his letter to the union leaders, confident that its contents had their tacit, if not their formal and public, support. For the first time the letter sketched out the company's broad aims: uninterrupted production, secure disputes procedures, lower manning and higher wage levels, new techniques and operating methods. And, also for the first time, it declared that if agreements on all these things had not been reached by 30 November, the company would suspend publication and dispense with its staff until they were.

These two meetings marked a crucial development in the company's thinking. They cleared the shutdown strategy over its first hurdle. The union leaders seemed ready to help. They had their own reasons, for the indiscipline at Times Newspapers was a challenge as much to their authority as to the company's, but that was all to the good. Hussey decided to reciprocate their apparent confidence in him. The company would involve them in every stage of its plans, getting their consent first and then, with their help, persuading the jostling multiplicity of union bargaining units inside the company to agree too.

The welcome the directors gave to the union leaders' expressions of support was understandable. But was it wise? Did the directors hear correctly, or did they hear what they wanted to hear?

The industrial drama which began to unfold at the Metropole and the Waldorf was, like any drama, about abstractions like power and principle, as well as more down-to-earth matters like jobs and money. But it was also a clash of institutions, personalities and styles, of generations, backgrounds and experience. It was a very human drama, and before raising the curtain on it we must take a closer look at the principal players, many of whom were present at those first two meetings.

The leaders of the print unions and the Times directors were a ripe sample of British industrial leadership in the late 1970s. To categorise them by their jobs, ranks and functions or by their starkly opposed roles as bargainers – as 'them' and 'us' – would be misleadingly simple. It would do less than justice to the real complexity of individuals and the relationships between them.

Nearly all had one thing in common. They were steeped in the print trade and had worked at scarcely anything else, though the trade unionists were more likely to have had a head start by being born into it. Men like Owen O'Brien and Bill Keys had fathers, brothers, sons in the trade or at one remove from it, in trade unionism. Only Mike Mander among the directors could claim the same, coming as he did from two generations of newspaper management on his father's side and two of journalists on his mother's.

There was one other experience the trade unionists shared which the directors did not. Being mostly older, they had all been in the forces in the Second World War. Remarkably, no fewer than four of the five trade unionists at the Metropole meeting – Keys, Ashton, Jackson, Dixon – had reached that most awesome of ranks, warrant officer first class or regimental sergeant-major. When the war was over each had gone back to the trade for a while before beginning the long, slow grind up the ladder of professional trade unionism which had taken them to the top in the 1970s, a grind in which the classic attributes of the sergeant-major – a powerful voice and a commanding presence – must have been useful.

As sergeant-majors do, each had his own distinctive style. Keys – good-humoured, ebullient, extrovert, a natural fixer, a politician in and out of politics; Jackson – a shade puritanical, very much the union boss, with a thoughtful turn of mind as befitted the leader of a small craft union; Dixon – easy-going, a man to take a drink with, a good platform speaker, ex-military policeman, and, like Jackson, highly conscious of his union's craft status; Ashton – a solid newspaperman who preferred the provinces to Fleet Street, fond of gliding, new to the upper ranks of trade unionism where journalists were still regarded as doubtful allies; O'Brien – an East Ender, perhaps the nicest man of the lot, eager to help get things right but, as it turned out, the least able to do so.

Of the directors, only Hussey and Hamilton had been in the war. Hussey, the son of a colonial civil servant, left Rugby to enter the Grenadier Guards, but he was able to spend a year at Oxford before joining up. His battle experience was short, five days at Anzio; it ended with Hussey, fearfully wounded, in the hands of the Germans, who amputated his leg under appalling conditions. Having returned to England, he went back to Oxford, where he spent years hovering between study and death, recovering sufficiently to take a job as a trainee with the *Daily Mail* in 1949. He worked his way up to a directorship of Associated Newspapers, coming over to the *Times* as chief executive in 1971. His marriage to Susan, the fifth daughter of the twelfth Earl Waldegrave, who later became a Woman of the Bedchamber to the Queen, brought Hussey into social circles more exalted than those of any of his colleagues and inspired distrust among the more class-conscious union officials.

Hamilton had been a young reporter on newspapers at Middlesbrough and Newcastle. He went to war with the Durham Light Infantry, rising to command a battalion, to be a member of Montgomery's staff and to win the Distinguished Service Order at Nijmegen. Montgomery personally invited him to stay on in the army, but Hamilton declined, not wishing to be a peace-time soldier, and went back to Newcastle at £8 a week. Within a month he had been summoned to London by Lord Kemsley, the chairman of the group which owned the Newcastle newspaper and also the *Sunday*

Times, to be his personal editorial assistant, and through the 1950s and 1960s he held high editorial posts in the Kemsley group. He laid the foundations of the modern *Sunday Times* and was its editor from 1961–6. After Roy Thomson had acquired the *Times* as well as the *Sunday Times* Hamilton became editor-in-chief of the two newspapers.

Hussey never brought the war up in conversation, though the damage it had done to his big frame must have been a constantly painful reminder. Beneath his cheery, almost Woosterish, upper-class manner, there seemed to lie a desperate urge to forget the past and get on with the future. He seemed to possess detachment, even optimism, as though whatever happened to him at the *Times* could not be worse than what had happened to him already.

Hamilton, by contrast, talked constantly about the war. A quiet, undemonstrative man, given to long pauses, it was patent that he felt deeply about the newspapers; but the dominant experience of his life still seemed to be battle. Privately or publicly, I was never to hear him speak without his finding some analogy between the war and events at Times Newspapers. It might be the style of leadership, which in industry, as in war, should be from the front; or the need for a chief executive, like a commanding officer, to get some sleep if he is to make the right decisions; or the importance of plans and briefings before moving any enterprise up to its startline.

Mike Mander and Dugal Nisbet-Smith, both in their early forties, had reached the board by quite different routes. Mander, a bachelor with bachelor tastes, self-effacing but decisive, had followed his father and Hussey into the management of Associated Newspapers, working his way up to become a director but growing disenchanted when the *Daily Sketch* was closed against his advice. The owner, Lord Rothermere, might have a perfect right to do as he pleased with his own newspaper, but that left little scope for an executive with ideas of his own. When a vacancy came up at Times Newspapers, Mander applied for it. Hussey, because he had worked with Mander at Associated, scrupulously declined to be at the interview, but Mander got the job all the same.

Nisbet-Smith, a burly and often abrasive New Zealander, had started out as a journalist, becoming frustrated with the prospects at the *Daily Express* and heading out to the West Indies to edit the

Barbados Advocate. While there, he met Cecil King, whose International Publishing Corporation (IPC) then owned a string of newspapers in the Commonwealth, as well as the *Daily Mirror* in London, around which King happened to be making one of his imperial tours. Nisbet-Smith served a stint in charge of the *Mirror*'s industrial relations in London and then went on to run IPC's highly profitable newspapers in Glasgow, from where Hussey had lured him.

Nisbet-Smith had joined the *Times* only the day before the meeting at the Metropole; Donald Cruickshank had joined only two months earlier. Both had been recruited by Hussey to fill gaps in the management structure, especially the one left by the death, on the first day of 1978, of Harvey Thompson, the general manager. And with them came a distinct change in management style, a change described by William Rees-Mogg as being from 'back-of-the-envelope' management to 'Harvard Business School'.

Rees-Mogg's description was not a literal one. Neither of the new directors had been to Harvard, though Cruickshank came nearest. In his mid-thirties (he was the youngest director), a tall, lean, fair-haired, patient man from Banffshire, he had been to Manchester Business School. A consultant by trade, he had been sought out by a firm of headhunters on a suggestion from Mander that the company needed someone with experience outside newspapers. But Rees-Mogg's phrase nevertheless conveys the essence of the change in management.

Harvey Thompson had been in the newspaper business since he left university. He had worked his way round all the departments of the *Manchester Guardian*, beginning with the editorial, and he knew the business inside out. At the *Times* he had known everything and everybody, kept the information in his head, written little down and made many decisions on his own without consulting the board. Shortly before he died, Hussey had joked to Mander that if they went, it would not matter much because their successors would find everything in order, but if Thompson went, a lot of important information would go with him. This left the new directors at a disadvantage. They did not know the Times or its people, and they did not have time to catch up before the crisis arrived. They also brought with them a professional style that was rational, objective, comprehensive and cool. These two factors – their newness and their new style –

were to have a significant effect on the company's handling of the dispute.

The two editors, Evans and Rees-Mogg, were also to make their marks on the dispute, though in quite different ways. Both were within a few months of their fiftieth birthdays, but otherwise they were as unalike as their two newspapers – Evans of the *Sunday Times* all energy and dash, and Rees-Mogg of the *Times* almost episcopal in his sobriety. The men matched their newspapers, but I have often wondered how they would have turned out if, as was considered in 1967, when both became editors, they had each got the other's newspaper. Would Rees-Mogg of the *Sunday Times* have developed a spring in his gait, and Evans of the *Times* become a shade austere?

But there cannot have been much doubt about who should get which newspaper when Hamilton moved up to be editor-in-chief, leaving the *Sunday Times* chair vacant, and Sir William Haley retired from the editorship of the *Times*. Evans, the son of a Manchester train driver, had reached London in his mid-thirties through the hard slog of provincial journalism, rising by way of Durham University and the Royal Air Force, through the *Manchester Evening News*, to become the editor of the *Northern Echo*, where he was spotted by Hamilton, who invited him to become his chief assistant.

Furiously hard-working, Evans set a pace which frequently baffled his journalists. Now we saw him, now we didn't – what on earth was he up to? He could demonstrate great patience, as he did in his ten-year fight to publish the inside story of the thalidomide drug tragedy, the coup for which he is probably best known. But he could be equally impatient, scurrying round the office, stopping here and there to rewrite a headline, bang out a leader, tear a page design apart, fire off a memo into his hungry recorder – nicknamed the 'monster' because of its prodigious appetite for his words – or argue the finer merits of a typeface or a news photo. He was the complete newspaper man, and nobody could be more desolate than he when an issue of his newspaper failed to reach all the people who wanted to buy it. And, perhaps for that very reason, he was instinctively shy about the shutdown strategy, over which he talked of resigning from the board.

Rees-Mogg, on the other hand, was one of the strategy's keenest supporters. A Catholic, the son of a solidly prosperous West Country family, he was educated at Charterhouse and Balliol, becoming president of the Oxford Union. He abandoned his aim of going into law when the editor of the *Financial Times*, Gordon Newton, offered him a job after spotting a profile in the Oxford magazine *Isis*, which revealed that Rees-Mogg, most unusually for an undergraduate, read the *Financial Times* every day.

Rees-Mogg had written of himself that he belonged to the 'comfortably off, middle-aged, English professional class', from among whom it was natural that people should find their 'worldly advisers'. And advice was what he gave daily through the leader columns of the *Times* – sweeping, magisterial, scholarly, sometimes constructed round a sporting metaphor, often taken from cricket. His support for the shutdown strategy was intellectually of a piece with the analysis his leaders presented of the condition of Britain: a country sluggish and run down, in need of a few sharp shocks to waken it to reality.

But if a shutdown made intellectual sense, the question still remained of whether it was practical. Was it the sort of scheme one of Rees-Mogg's 'worldly advisers' would recommend? Was Hussey right in thinking that he had found a special harmony with the union leaders at the April meetings?

Those meetings gave the directors the confidence they needed to go ahead with their 'big bang' strategy. Whether the meetings justified their confidence is hard to say. No record of the meetings has been kept and there are as many versions of what was said as there are participants willing to talk about them. Perhaps the harmony was an illusion, conjured up by the relaxed atmosphere of comfortable hotel rooms. I have sometimes wondered if it was a relic of the war. Now the sergeant-majors were promoted. They could get their feet under the same mess table as the officers and sort out their common problems like old comrades. This may be fanciful, though there was certainly to be a real difference of tone between the old soldiers and the younger generation of managers and union officials, who were altogether more hard-nosed and less sentimental, more professional, maybe, but narrower and less forgiving. And if the harmony was not that of old comrades, then it was an illusion built on something equally fanciful. For it did not last long. Back in their offices, among their own people, the union leaders quickly trimmed the enthusiasm

Hussey thought they had shown and began tacking to windward of their members.

They were not the only ones to change their moods and minds. Important though the feelings and personalities of individuals were, none was a free agent. The Times directors and the union leaders were integral parts of their own organisations, creatures, to a degree, of the institutions which created them. To understand events at Times Newspapers, it is necessary to know something more about those institutions.

2
UNITY
IN
DISCORD

On the last day the *Times* was published before it shut down, a harassed television researcher asked me how far back in time he ought to go to get to the root of it all. Without thinking twice, I said: 'Why not 1476?' It was not a very practical date for television, but it was not ridiculous either. 1476 was the year in which Caxton set up the first English printing press at Westminster Abbey, and the printing trade has flourished in London ever since. Its labour organisations – the chapels and the unions – have been part of the trade almost from the start, giving them strong claims to be the oldest surviving forms of labour organisation in Britain. And the problems with which they were to grapple at Times Newspapers – an immense, multi-coloured jigsaw of jobs and pay, skills and technology – were problems they had been handling since the dawn of industrial capitalism. The unions at Times Newspapers did not spring up overnight in order to baffle and confound the management. They had been ripening for centuries.

Chapels are, and always have been, the bedrock of printing trade unionism. Quite where the name came from is obscure. Perhaps it can be traced to Caxton's start at Westminster Abbey. Experts disagree. At any rate, there seems to be a touch of parody in the name chosen for the elected leader, the 'father of the chapel', an exotic title for someone who elsewhere in industry would be a humdrum shop steward.

At first, the chapel was a kind of self-regulating workshop club. It would fine members for being drunk at work, then use its collection of fines so that all members could get drunk together. Printing houses were small and technically simple, and a single chapel contained the whole staff. From an early date they accumulated elaborate rules and rituals. Benjamin Franklin worked in a London print shop in 1725. His master wanted to shift him from one job to another, from the press to the composing room. The compositors demanded that he pay an entry fee – a 'bien venu' – but he refused, having already paid one when he joined the press room. But so many mysterious tricks were played on him that he paid up for the sake of peace.*

At this stage, the chapel was not a trade union or part of one. Industry was still heavily regulated by Parliament and the guilds, and the modern distinctions between master and man, employer and employee were not yet established. But the perennial preoccupations of the trade – money, jobs and craft exclusiveness – had already long been fixed. Scarcely more than a hundred years after Caxton set up shop, the Court of the Stationers' Company in 1587 issued a characteristic order, limiting to 1250 the number of copies that could be printed from one setting of a book. Any more, and the book had to be set in type all over again. The purpose of the order was to make work for men who might otherwise be idle – an early example of a restrictive practice perhaps (or, as printers might have called it then and certainly would now, protective practice).

But as regulation of industry fell into disuse in the eighteenth century, print workers felt themselves more and more exposed to the chances of the market. High wages and craft exclusiveness were no longer enforced on print shops by the state. And a chapel on its own could do little to replace the state's authority. A chapel might keep a tight grip on conditions in its own house, but if the customer could go down the road to another house, where the chapel's grip was weaker and the cost of print lower, nothing had been achieved. The only answer was a 'union' between chapels, and unions – probably the first authentic ones in Britain – were what print workers began to organise in the last quarter of the eighteenth century. In 1785 the first print union made its first deal. Compositors agreed a scale of piecework prices with employers, and scales that are its direct heirs are still in operation in Fleet Street today.

It was not only employers who competed, however. Workmen competed for jobs too. Control over who works in the trade was (and

* *Memoirs of the Life and Writings of Benjamin Franklin* (London, 1818), vol. I, p. 69.

is to this day a prime obsession of print workers, for unless the supply of labour was kept within strict limits, the price of the labour could not be set high and the jobs could not be made secure. Men willing to work for less than the standard rate were just as much of a threat as any hard-faced employer.

The apprenticeship has always been at the heart of the system of labour control. As early as 1576, men who had not served their time as apprentices and been duly qualified as journeymen were angrily denounced as 'foreigners' – a word with a fine ring of craft chauvinism which would not have sounded out of place in the Times dispute, when 'foreigners' were as much an issue as they had ever been.

The period of apprenticeship was fixed at seven years in the sixteenth century – the same term that was served by many compositors working at the *Times* today. The standing of a time-served printer has always been high, but the seven-year apprenticeship stint at very low wages was a powerful deterrent to would-be journeymen. And although the length of an apprenticeship was a handy way to keep down numbers, it was an ambiguous ally of the print worker. Since it seems never actually to have taken seven years to produce a competent craftsman, an apprentice might in reality find himself undercutting the very same journeymen whose ranks he was struggling to join. At any moment an excess of apprentices was a threat to the present and future well-being of men in the trade, and even when the unions were able to control recruitment, it was, and still is, a headache to settle the numbers.

Not surprisingly, the Fleet Street craftsman identifies strongly with his union. He is indebted to it for his apprenticeship, his job, his rate of pay and all his other conditions of work. It runs its own labour exchanges, through which he can find work, and a rudimentary welfare system, which is prosperous enough to look after him well at least when he is in dispute. By comparison, the employer is almost a bystander in the craftsman's scheme of things. Even if he entirely disagrees with what his union is doing, the craftsman is unlikely to stretch his disagreement too far, for he knows that his union's rule book gives it the right to deprive him of his membership card, his only passport to a job.

These are the disciplines of the old-style craft unions, the NGA and Slade, whose members' main work is in the production of print and of pictures respectively. But the ancient simplicities of the single-chapel Caxtonian print shop have long gone from Fleet Street. A big national newspaper is a complex business, part production unit, part commercial house and part journalism, and it requires more than the traditional printing skills to produce. It needs electricians and engineers, librarians and drivers and dozens more. These employees are necessary to newspapers, but they are not exclusive to them: a secretary may sell her services in any office in central London, not just in Fleet Street. Among people like these there is not the same long experience, starting with apprenticeship, that binds the individual to his union. Nor does the union leader have the same purchase over his rank and file. The threat of expulsion is apt to be empty when made against a clerk who may find a job as good or better just around the corner and outside the trade.

Union influence is still powerful among newspaper employees whose skills are not those of the traditional craftsmen and who belong to other unions. But it is differently focused. The closed shop compels most Fleet Street employees to be union members, but for many non-craftsmen membership comes after they get their jobs, not before. Loyalties are centred on branches or chapels, which in turn makes branch and chapel officials highly independent of central union authority, able to act very much as they please. While central authority may be strong in the NGA and Slade, it can be very tenuous in general unions like Natsopa or Sogat.

It is the same with yet a third category of union, those which are not print unions at all but whose members are present to service buildings and machinery wherever manufacturing takes place – electricians, engineers and carpenters. Outside the mainstream of their own unions, they too focus loyalty on branch or chapel.

The NUJ shares many of the characteristics of the other unions, but none of them very fervently. Among organised Fleet Street workers journalist are unique. They live in two economic worlds, one in which their union negotiates minimum rates and regular rises all round, and another in which they bargain for themselves directly with their editor. Since a deal with the editor can hardly fail to be better than the union rate, the journalist pins his highest hopes on himself and his own market power. There are closed NUJ shops in Fleet Street, though not at Times Newspapers, but there is also a rival union, the Institute of Journalists, to which a minority of journalists belong. Journalists' interest in their union is rarely fired by anything other than the annual wage round. Such thin union loyalties as they have are focused on their chapel. The branch and the national union are seen as remote nuisances, to be tolerated rather than obeyed.

There is another reason why Fleet Street journalists make unenthusiastic trade unionists. Journalism is more fun than trade unionism, and trade union duties take up time that could be better spent on making a career. At the *Sunday Times* competition for chapel office is less than keen, and chapel officers have often had to be elected in their absence because all those who were actually at the chapel election meeting refused to be elected.

In other unions the opposite is more likely to be the case. For many employees the only escape from being what they are – electricians or compositors, say – is into a career in management or the union. Fleet Street provides more opportunities for a union career than most industries. Gray's Inn Road houses an extraordinary number of people working full-time as shop stewards with their own offices and telephones and sometimes a secretary too, all paid for by the company. As a way of life, trade unionism can offer a lot more than working at the trade to those with ambition and a taste for politics.

But all the chapels of all the unions, whatever their style or character, have caught one habit of mind from the original craft unions – the habit of exclusiveness. Just as the craft unions repel 'foreigners', so other unions repel their outsiders. Each union and chapel marks out for itself a set of functions to be performed only by its own members; each throws an invisible boundary wire around its own territory; and each works its enclosed and private patch for all it can harvest in jobs and money. By common consent each chapel can do as it pleases inside its own boundary, even if that means taking action that stops the newspaper. The cardinal sin is to invade the patch of another union.

This sense of territory runs wide and deep. One example will show how and why the habit, being so profitable, is so infectious. Until a hundred years ago the whole of a newspaper – advertisements as well as editorial copy – was set in type by the newspaper's own compositors. Then along came the advertising campaign and with it the display advertisement, which today may take up a whole page ex-

tolling, say, a new motor car or an airline's fares. If the same advertisement were to appear in several newspapers, it made obvious sense
to have it prepared only once in one place, and to meet this need a
whole new subsidiary industry of specialised houses grew up around
Fleet Street. But if whole pages were to be set outside a newspaper's
own composing room, what price the territorial integrity of the newspaper's composing room chapels, which had been assumed to imply
the right to fill all the pages of the paper with type?

In 1894 a settlement of this dilemma, wholly characteristic of Fleet
Street, was reached. The display advertisements would be set in the
new specialised houses, but the compositors at the newspaper in
which the advertisements were placed would be paid as if it were
they who had set them. Thus work was done in the way the advertisers wanted, but the territorial rights of the compositors had
been respected in an ingenious formula that also gave them less work
for more pay. 'Fat' it was called, and fat it still is today.

By dozens of schemes and deals like this the print unions have
tried to build little islands of stability for their members in a turbulent
market ocean. But, though highly conservative, print trade unionism
is never quite static. Technical change and union politics are always
forcing the structure into new shapes. The genealogies of the print
unions reflect this restlessness, giving them the look of dissolute
dynasties, strewn with forced alliances and messy separations. With
its official history the National Union of Printing, Bookbinding and
Paper Workers provides a pull-out family tree of its own complex
ancestry, which shows the oldest member of the family to be the
Journeymen Bookbinders of London, born in 1786. Fifty-four years
later their three lodges combined into the London Consolidated
Lodge of Journeymen Bookbinders. Six years after that the day-
working bookbinders formed a breakaway. But in 1911 they returned
to the fold and, together with the Vellum Binders' Society (born 1823)
and the Machine Rulers, formed a new union which lasted for ten
years until it threw in its lot with cutters, warehousemen, paper
workers and several more.

That is by no means the end of the story; having metamorphosed
several times more, the union became the present-day Sogat, which
might have disappeared into history too, had not a merger between

Sogat and Natsopa in the 1960s come unstuck. But this is enough to convey the sense of ceaseless grouping and regrouping that has gone on among print unions as new trades have emerged and old ones declined in a continuous evolution that has been robbed of its logic of natural selection only by the irruption of obscure and mostly forgotten political and personal feuds. Even during the Times Newspapers shutdown a merger was attempted between the NGA and Slade, but it was rejected by a ballot of Slade members in spite of – or perhaps because of – being recommended by the union's leaders.

Preserving rafts of stability in an industry subject to constant creeping modification and rare bursts of radical change is not easy. It means fighting off other unions every bit as much as management, and it can lead to some long and bitter hostilities. In 1913, for instance, Natsopa made a small but significant change in its name. It inserted an 'and' between the last two words of its title, the National Society of Operative Printers' Assistants, as a way of signalling a claim to be regarded as craftsmen and not just craftsmen's assistants. But it did not work. The craftsmen kept the best jobs and a Natsopa machine assistant in Fleet Street cannot hope to jump the barrier into NGA territory and become a machine manager, however competent he may be to do the job. He is forever doomed to stay where he is, and it rankles still in Natsopa.

The NGA may have been able to throw off a challenge from Natsopa in 1913, but the challenge posed by the new photo-composing technology bought by Times Newspapers in the 1970s was an altogether tougher proposition. Of all the invasions of union territory contained in the company's plans, this was potentially by far the most serious. As the NGA saw it from the start, if the company succeeded in introducing the new systems, the implications for the union and its members were tremendous. Times Newspapers would have achieved a sort of Normandy landing. It would have established a beach-head from which the whole industry might break out and overrun long-held NGA ground. In the end it could even destroy the union.

Photo-composition as such was not new. The idea of creating type by photographic means rather than in metal had been around for almost as long as moving film. A union historian, writing in 1949, said that it was already regarded 'with not a little trepidation'.* But it had taken time to evolve, and in practice it had been absorbed by the provincial press and the general printing trade without much trouble. If Times Newspapers had simply wanted to replace its hot-metal composing room with photo-composition (or 'cold type'), it would not have had much trouble either. But the system it had bought in California went one stage further. It linked photo-composing equipment through computers to terminals which could be located outside the composing room, on journalists' desks or in the tele-ad department, where classified advertisements are taken over the telephone. Seated before one of the new terminals, a journalist could perform two jobs at once. He could write his story on the terminal keyboard and, once he was satisfied with it, he could instruct the computer to have the story set in type. The same keystroke that wrote the journalist's copy also prepared the type. There would be no need for a second pair of hands to dance upon a second keyboard.

In the history of printing this was truly revolutionary. For four out of the five centuries during which there has been printing in Britain type was set by hand. The compositor picked each letter from the case in front of him and added it to the type in the galley he held in his hand. Various machines were tried out, but it was not until the Linotype reached Newcastle from New York in 1889 that the right mechanical formula was found. Members of the NGA – or rather of its precedessors, the Typographical Association and the London Society of Compositors – were dismayed. The new machines might so speed up the business of typesetting that far fewer men would be needed; and operating it might be classed as unskilled labour which could be done by men (and even women) who had not served an apprenticeship. In the event, the union managed to keep the machines for the exclusive use of its members. And the Linotype helped to cheapen print, so that there were more publications and, by 1900, more compositors at work than ever before.

From a union point of view, this was a fairy-tale of technical advance, just how these things ought to be. But the new Times systems were altogether more menacing. Nobody ever expected a journalist to write his copy directly on to a Linotype, which was –

---

* A. E. Musson, *The Typographical Association* (Oxford, 1954), p. 522.

and is – a monstrous, noisy Victorian typewriter. It would have been impossible. There had to be a second pair of hands and a second keystroke with the Linotype, and it did not threaten the territorial integrity of the composing room as the only place in a newspaper office where type could be set. But the new terminals could be put anywhere in the office or even outside it, and they could be used by anybody who could work a typewriter.

In fact, the company did not intend to abolish the composing room. For a while at least, most material would continue to be written by one person and set in type by another. There would be fewer jobs for compositors (45 per cent fewer), but that would come about entirely through the switch-over from hot-metal machines to the much faster photo-composing equipment. It was the equipment and not the journalist that would eliminate most of the NGA's jobs. But to the NGA that was not the point; what mattered was that there should always be a second keystroke and that it should always be made by someone who belonged to the NGA and to no other union. It was to defend the interests of the men who performed the typesetting function that the NGA came into being, and that was what the union was still primarily in business to do. It was not about to surrender that function to Times journalists. For if it did, it might be starting a long slide that would lead to the disappearance not only of jobs but of the union itself.

As a matter of self-preservation the NGA saw good reasons for keeping the new technology at bay. But the NGA was not the only body with a vested interest in the *status quo*. The management's plans involved a reduction in staff in most sections, which must also lead to reductions in union memberships. Since union and union income at every level – chapel, branch, national union – depends entirely on membership, any loss of numbers must mean a loss of power and income. Nor is a union simply an abstraction, the sum of its members' aspirations. It is an organisation which provides jobs and careers. At every step, therefore, the management plans were sure to be tested not only by the measure of what the staff wanted, but also by how well they fitted in with the policies of unions and the ambitions of union officials.

The Times management had to reckon with a work force whose natural conservatism was reinforced by a trade-union system of dazzling complexity. There were at Gray's Inn Road in 1978 eight unions, divided into sixty-five chapels, representing some 4250 staff. Each chapel was zealous for its own traditional rights and jealous of those of all the others. Each insisted on negotiating for its own members exclusively, while at the same time keeping an eye on all the others to make sure they did not steal an advantage. Any proposal the management made to one chapel had first to be weighed for its impact on the others.

To add to the complexity, two events of the previous twenty years had had serious consequences for whatever homogeneity the work force might have been expected to maintain. The first occurred in 1961, when the *Daily Telegraph* ended its contract to print the *Sunday Times*. The contract had been a long-standing arrangement between the two Berry brothers who owned the two newspapers, from one of whom, Lord Kemsley, Roy Thomson had recently bought the *Sunday Times*. Thomson seems to have offended the other Berry, Lord Hartwell, by proposing to buy the *Telegraph* from him. Whatever the reason, Hartwell gave Thomson the shortest possible notice to quit, leaving Thomson to equip his own press room in short order and to recruit a scratch staff for Saturday nights. The new staff had to be casual workers because Thomson could not offer them jobs on the other nights of the week, and, in the management's view, the staff had never settled in to become a loyal part of a loyal team.

The second event was, if anything, even more traumatic. After being published for nearly two hundred years from the same place, Printing House Square, between the Thames and St Paul's Cathedral, the *Times* was moved in the mid-1970s to a new building in Gray's Inn Road on a site next to the *Sunday Times* office called New Printing House Square. Being in the City, the *Times*'s old office stood on valuable property, and the company also hoped to make economies by merging some of its activities in the two neighbouring buildings, which were linked by a bridge. But, psychologically at least, the move had not been a success. The chapels of each newspaper watched one another with suspicion, each blaming the intrusion of the other for unsettling its previous harmonies. The newspapers' new closeness gave their chapels opportunities to make comparisons, which inevitably turned into claims. And the staffs of both newspapers disliked each other's management and style. The weight of these events cannot be measured, but they contributed powerfully to the sense of unease which underlay the attitudes of the whole work force in the late 1970s.

The slow maturing in its ways of Fleet Street and its unions has produced a style that must seem bizarre to a stranger but is as natural as paper and ink to those in the trade. The Fleet Street print worker and his union may be radical in their talk, but they are intensely conservative when it comes to their own affairs. A printer may wish for the overthrow of the capitalist system, but meanwhile things had better stay very much as they are. He is dedicated to his demarcations, to preserving that patch of the printing process that has been marked out for him. (A journalist, drunk, once threw up in the lobby of the *Sunday Times* building, in front of another employee who had only just finished mopping the floor. Pulling himself together, the journalist borrowed the mop to clean up, but he was stopped in the friendliest possible fashion when he began mopping beyond the area which it was the other man's job to clean. It did not matter if the rest was left messy: that was somebody else's work.)

This sense of exclusiveness requires a running battle with the management and with other unions. No union and no chapel may pry into the affairs of any other. (I once sat as a journalists' representative on a committee that was supposed to bring together all the chapels in the *Sunday Times*, the federated house chapel. Most of the time we talked about canteen prices, because we could all agree that they should not go up. There was little else we could agree on or even discuss, since any subject of real interest, like pay or production, was held to be a matter for individual chapels and was therefore taboo.)

Print workers are endowed with a subtle but profound sense of hierarchy. Their notions of order, as defined by skills and differentials, are as complete as any aristocrat's. They can show a snobbery that would put a duke to shame. (One senior craft union official once expressed to me his contempt for a non-craft union in this philosophical reminiscence: 'I am a child of the thirties,' he said. 'I was brought up to believe that the greatest thing we could do was to liberate India from the British Empire. We believed that Indians were fine fellows. And then I went to India in the services during the war. And, do you know, I found I didn't like them. They weren't clean. They were nasty, a rabble. And do you know,' he finished, 'that is what I think of Natsopa.')

And, finally, the Fleet Street printer's feeling towards his employer is one of high disdain born of the power he has to thwart and ignore him. So powerful had the print unions become that, as Times management saw it, they had begun to replace management in its own function. The unions hired people, allocated work, determined shifts and holidays and even totted up their earnings at the end of the week. Not the least of the Times ambitions was to seize back some of this lost managerial power.

But unions do not grow in a vacuum. They are above all negotiators, and their characters are shaped as much by the employers with whom they negotiate as by anything they choose for themselves. The unions and chapels of Fleet Street are what they are because of their long entanglement with the newspaper proprietors. If the print unions at Times Newspapers had their peculiarities and faults, then the newspaper employers had done as much as anybody to create them.

3
ABSENTEE LANDLORDS

Fleet Street is more than the geographical centre of Britain's national press. It also holds out a promise of freedom and success for journalists and of wealth and power for their proprietors: it is a street of adventure or a street of shame. But at the same time it is the focus of the only real manufacturing industry left in central London.

Dreams of journalists may often clash with the whims of proprietors, but the fancies of both are brought down to earth by industrial reality. Newspapers must make money to survive, and to make money they must keep on terms with the unions whose members produce them. If those unions are turbulent, the proprietors have helped to make them so. The two sides of this industry bear an uncommon resemblance to one another. The employers are no less buccaneering and opportunistic than the unions, and the genealogies of their publishing houses no less quaint and eccentric.

From the similarity of their names, people often believe that the *Times* and the *Sunday Times* were born of the same family. They were not. For most of their long lives they have lived apart. The *Times* was founded in 1788 and the *Sunday Times* in 1822, when its owner, Henry White, having tried without much success to sell his sheet as the *New Observer* and the *Independent Observer*, decided to ape the *Times*'s title and cash in on its success.

The *Sunday Times* has had a whole string of owners, including two women (one a Sassoon) and a consortium among whose members were Sir Basil Zaharoff, the legendary arms salesman, the original 'merchant of death', Dr Jameson of the notorious Jameson raid and a chairman of the Tory Party, Sir Arthur Steel-Maitland. It found a more settled existence when it was bought during the First World War by the Berry brothers, one of whom became Lord Kemsley and retained and built up the paper, while the other became Lord Camrose and went on to run the *Daily Telegraph*. Ownership of the *Times* has been more constant. The family of the founder, John Walter, remained in charge for more than a hundred years until the paper was sold to Lord Northcliffe and then to Major (later Lord) Astor.

The *Sunday Times*'s succession of owners suggests its character, which is squarely within the tradition of English Sunday newspapers: adventurous, sensational, sometimes radical, a shade raffish, always in search of novelty and change. The *Times* has always been and still is an altogether different beast, a pioneer technically and editorially, high-minded but reticent, almost clerically restrained in its demeanour. The *Times* was the first newspaper to bring steam power to printing. Almost single-handed, it created the idea of the newspaper as an authoritative organ of record and opinion. It has always seen itself as much more than a commercial enterprise, as a necessary part of the nation's public life, almost like Parliament, the Church and the Crown. Writing in the last but one edition of the *Times* before it shut down, the editor found that he had something in common with the Pope, 'an unqualified responsibility to protect the integrity and continuity of our institutions'. It was, he said, 'the first duty of an Editor of the *Times* not to be the last one.' Few journalists would dare to speak so reverentially of their own jobs.

It was through an accident of business that these two very different newspapers came together at last. Roy Thomson, an elderly Canadian publisher, bought the *Sunday Times* in 1959 and the *Times* in 1966. He was in the market for other national newspapers as well, but, as it happened, these were the two he wanted to have whose proprietors were ready to sell.

Thomson's was one of the strangest success stories of the age. He came to Britain to buy the Edinburgh newspaper, the *Scotsman*, in 1953, when he was already in his sixtieth year, owned sixteen newspapers and a group of radio stations in Canada and was rich enough for his own modest tastes. But his wife had recently died; he had been frustrated in an attempt to enter the Canadian Parliament; and he was looking around for something new to do. With the *Scotsman* as his base, he went on to establish commercial television in Scotland, thus acquiring for himself, in his own celebrated phrase, 'a licence to print money'. Then he let it be known to anybody who owned newspapers that he was interested in buying. In 1959 Lord Kemsley took him at his word and sold him the *Sunday Times* and a chain of provincial newspapers in order to preserve his own fortune against death duties. And in 1966 Lord Astor sold him the *Times*, because it was losing money and needed a revivifying injection of cash. Thomson went on to promote the Yellow Pages telephone directories, the largest travel company in Britain and, with the Americans Paul Getty and Armand Hammer, the development of the Piper and Claymore oil fields in the North Sea, which might have been called his second licence to print money.

It was an extraordinary late blooming in the last twenty years of a long life, and it certainly made Thomson very rich indeed. But, for a rich man, he inspired a good deal of affection and surprisingly little resentment. Money was his passion, but in him it seemed curiously innocent, like a hobby. That was how he struck me the only time I met him. He had sent for a reporter to come to his room, designed for him by Lord Snowdon on the top floor of the *Sunday Times* office, because he thought he might be on to a good story for the paper, and I was asked to go. He had two friends with him, but it soon became obvious that they had no story. So, politely but briskly, Thomson ended the meeting. As he was showing us out, he paused for a moment and peered through his thick pebble glasses at a picture on the wall. 'What do you think that is?' he asked. Although the picture was not photographically exact, it clearly showed an elephant in long grass, and one of us said so. 'You're right,' said Thomson. 'Most people think it's an atomic bomb explosion. I don't look at it very often, but it's by Sidney Nolan, and every time I do look at it I think, well, it's gone up in value since the last time I looked.' He twinkled cheerfully, seeming to enjoy adding to his reputation for meanness, and it was impossible to dislike his candour.

By the time of his death in 1976 Roy (by now Lord) Thomson had constructed a huge conglomerate empire in publishing, travel and oil, of which the *Times* and the *Sunday Times* were certainly the most famous parts but far from the most profitable. In 1977 the two newspapers together made a trading profit of £1.9 million. It was a good year for them, the first one since Thomson bought the *Times* that it had been in the black. But this profit was meagre enough when set against the £4 millions from travel, £10 millions from the provincial newspapers and a staggering £82 millions from oil.

The business Roy Thomson left behind was being rapidly transformed by oil money. It did not look at all the same as it had ten years before. Through the 1960s Thomson had been eager to expand beyond his original newspaper and television interests, in both of which he felt vulnerable. Both were subject to the fluctuations of the economy and of advertisement revenue. His television interests were liable to political interference that could end his control in Scotland – as was indeed to happen. And the newspapers were already prone to union disruption. He therefore sought out new opportunities in publishing books and magazines and in travel. Oil was business of a different order. It was not Thomson's idea to get into it. He was approached by Getty and Hammer, who were having great trouble in finding the British partner they needed to stake a claim to North Sea oil. Thomson persuaded them to bear most of the initial risk but by the late 1970s the speculation was paying off in a torrent of cash.

But the torrent would not last for ever. The Piper and Claymore fields in which Thomson had a 20 per cent interest must dry up one day. Now there was a new problem – to find a safe, sound home for all that oil money, some venture in which it could be well invested to sustain the Organisation into the 1990s. Various ideas were considered. Perhaps the Organisation might branch out in a new direction, as it had done in the 1960s when it went into travel. It could buy Woolworth's and enter the retail trade. But in the end Thomson decided to stay in the business his Organisation knew: publishing first of all, but travel and natural resources as well.

This basic decision implied another. If the Organisation were to concentrate primarily on publishing, it could not confine itself to Britain, where it was already running up against the limits of expansion. It owned so large a share of the country's newspapers that monopoly laws would prevent it from buying more. Once all the money that could usefully be spent on the British businesses had been spent, it was to North America, whose markets were vast and whose politics were as stable as anywhere in the world, that Thomson looked. The Thomson Organisation was wound up and replaced by a new company, Thomson British Holdings, answerable to a new holding company, the International Thomson Organisation (ITO), based in Toronto, the home town of the second Lord Thomson, Kenneth, who owned 81 per cent of the holding company's shares.

Whatever the commercial wisdom of this move, it undoubtedly had an important effect on the negotiations at Times Newspapers. It seemed yet another in a series of changes whose effect was to put an ever-increasing distance between the newspapers and their proprietor; and it confused the structure of management authority.

Roy Thomson and his directors had once inhabited the *Sunday Times* building, the name of which had been changed from Kemsley House to Thomson House when Thomson bought it. Even if we did not know him personally, his short, stout, black-hatted figure was a familiar one around the office, and his Rolls-Royce, numbered 1 RHT, was constantly at the front door. Then he took the Thomson House name to a new head office in Stratford Place, off Oxford Street. But Thomson continued to keep his headquarters in England and to live there himself. Now ownership had been transferred to Roy's son, Kenneth, who had taken the headquarters across the Atlantic. And though Kenneth kept a flat in London, he preferred to spend most of his time in Toronto.

To the staff and the unions this was distinctly unsettling. We – and the world – might believe our newspapers were of great importance, but in the perspective of our proprietor we were only a small, remote, unruly province in a great corporate empire. We were tenants in the estate of an absentee landlord, left in the charge of uncaring stewards.

There was a paradox in the nature of Kenneth Thomson's ownership. Technically, he was in the position of an old-fashioned proprietor. Although Lord Astor still kept 15 per cent of the shares of Times Newspapers, Thomson effectively controlled the rest through his control of the ITO. 'National' directors – a banker, a trade unionist, an historian – had been appointed to the board of Times Newspapers when Roy Thomson bought the *Times* in an effort to safeguard the public interest in the newspaper's independence. But they acted as little more than advisers throughout the dispute. There was nothing to stop Kenneth Thomson from behaving as imperiously as any Beaverbrook or Northcliffe had done in their time, and to the staff that was exactly how he did behave when he closed down the newspapers. Only a proprietor with no one but himself to please could decide to spend millions in this way. And not even the most authoritarian of the breed had ever shut his newspaper deliberately or for so long.

But Kenneth Thomson did not otherwise behave like a proprietor. He delegated the handling of Times problems to the directors of Times Newspapers and of Thomson British Holdings. To newspaper people, used to looking proprietors directly in the eye, this was highly confusing. As things were set up at Times Newspapers, it was difficult to know whose eye to look into. Was it the eye of the chairman of Times Newspapers, Sir Denis Hamilton, who was also the editor-in-chief of the two newspapers? Or was it Duke Hussey's, the chairman of Times Newspapers executive board, which was in charge of the daily business of the newspapers? Or was it the eye of Gordon Brunton, Thomson's chief executive? Or even that of Lord Thomson, the owner, thousands of miles away in Canada?

This structure of authority may have looked fine on paper. It may have fitted sensible theories of good corporate practice, according to which local directors are left to run their part of the business with only occasional nudges from the top. But it increased enormously the management's problems of credibility. For it always seemed to a union negotiator that he had not quite reached the end of the road. If a junior manager said no, might there not be a different answer from Hussey, and if not from Hussey, then from Hamilton, or Brunton, or perhaps Lord Thomson himself? The structure was unfamiliar and hard to get to grips with, and to the staff and the unions the confusion inevitably presented itself as a question of personalities. It would never have happened with the old man, union leaders often said to me; it would all have been different with Roy. Since they could not see Roy and did not see Kenneth, their recriminations fell on those nearer home, on Hussey and Dugal Nisbet-Smith, who were cast as the villains of the piece.

This may have been as unfair to Kenneth Thomson as to Hussey and Nisbet-Smith. But it was unavoidable, given the elusive nature of authority within an organisation which somehow combined the old prerogatives of the proprietor with the new imperatives of a modern corporate management. And the staff's sense of being in a kind of limbo, caught between the different tides running within the organisation to which they belonged, did in fact reflect a real truth about their place in that organisation. The millions of its own money which the Thomson family put into the newspapers before and after the shutdown were proof enough of its devotion to them. But the fact was that the two newspapers were no longer the centrepieces of their owner's concern, as they had been for previous owners like the Walters or Lord Kemsley. They had become, rather, the flagships of an organisation, a high-visibility operation which could be extremely useful to a business with a lot of money to spend in the publishing industry.

Thomson's was not yet a household name in that industry. Big though his organisation was, its name was not proof of respectability or achievement. But the *Times* of London stood for both and more. When Callaghan and Company, a substantial family-owned Chicago firm of law publishers, came on the market it was very helpful in establishing Thomson's credentials as a bidder to be able to say that he owned Times Newspapers. A takeover was agreed in March 1979, after Callaghan's representatives had been entertained in the dining-room at New Printing House Square.

Novel though it may have been to the staff, the place of Times Newspapers within the Thomson family interests was, by the late 1970s, comparable with that of almost all the rest of the national press within other corporate empires. The *Daily Mail* might still be owned by the Harmsworth family who had founded it, but the family's interests now extended far beyond the national press, into the North Sea and elsewhere. The *Daily Mirror* was now part of the great Reed International group of companies. The *Daily Express* belonged to Trafalgar House, a property and shipping conglomerate. The *Observer* had been bought by Atlantic Richfield, an American oil company. Only the *Telegraph* newspapers still formed an old-fashioned, independent publishing house under the control of a genuinely old-fashioned editor-proprietor, Lord Hartwell.

In Hussey's view, the unions themselves had been at least partly responsible for the change of ownership. The unions had driven the old proprietors so hard that they had had to sell out or find other sources of income to keep their papers going. But was this an advantage to the press? Hussey set out his own doubts in a remarkably frank letter to James Prior, then the Tory spokesman on labour affairs, a month after the company's first meeting with the union general secretaries. He wrote:

One of the consequences of union ill discipline has been the changing

pattern of newspaper ownership. Now, individual companies have
been steadily eliminated – Kemsley, Cadbury [owners of the defunct
News Chronicle], Aitken [of the *Daily Express*], Astor [of the
Observer]. Instead newspapers are very small parts of very large and,
in some cases, multi-national concerns, i.e. Trafalgar House, Atlantic
Richfield, the Thomson Organisation, Reeds, Pearson [which owns
the *Financial Times*].

It was, he thought, 'an example of where union intransigence has
brought its own reaction in terms of more powerful proprietors'. The
new owners, Hussey implied, were better equipped to stand up to the
unions and fight back. But was this a step forward? Hussey had his
doubts.

> Whether this is in the long-term interests of the press is disputable
> because, of course, whatever you may say against the individual
> proprietors, they did know all about the freedom of the press. What
> view the top boards of multi-national companies will take of that sort
> of issue we don't know yet.

The question Hussey raised is still unanswered. We still do not
know how these boards would react in a political crisis. Would they
compel their editors to toe a particular line against their own beliefs?
It has not happened so far. At Times Newspapers Evans and Rees-
Mogg have been left scrupulously alone. While other directors may
be abused at board meetings about failures in production or distribution, the editors are never charged with poor journalism or with
eccentricity in their editorial opinions.

The motives of the new owners remain hard to discern. But what
is clear is that they have not used their resources to tackle the unions
in the way that Hussey's letter envisaged. The opposite is more
nearly true. They have used their money to give a fresh lease on life
to the very same costly labour practices that forced the old proprietors to sell or transform their businesses.

Fleet Street's labour problems are hardly a secret. They have been
studied to the point of tedium by three Royal Commissions, the
Economist Intelligence Unit, the National Board for Prices and Incomes and countless other pundits over the last thirty years. Each
report has given much the same verdict, that the industry is over-
manned, over-paid and, more recently, plain out-of-date in its

technology. In the 1960s such gloomy analyses had led to the fear that Fleet Street could no longer collectively generate enough income from newspaper sales and advertisement revenue to cover the cost of producing all its titles with the inflated staffs the print unions imposed on them. One or more titles would have to die, as Roy Thomson had frequently prophesied. At that time newspapers were unpopular properties. When Thomson offered to buy the *Times* in 1966 the Government, reluctant to let him add any more to his inventory of newspapers, kept him waiting to see if another buyer would appear; but none did.

By the 1970s the climate had mysteriously changed. When the *Express* and the *Observer* appeared to be on the edge of extinction eager corporations arrived to buy them up. Newspapers, it seemed, led a charmed life. They could defy the ordinary laws of commercial gravity and still survive. All the gloomy predictions had turned out to be untrue. Who could blame the unions and the chapels for failing to learn the lessons expounded by those wise prophets whose forecasts of extinction had proved to be so wrong?

Under the new owners Fleet Street's bad habits continued and even intensified. Newspapers are inherently vulnerable to lightning action by unions. Tuesday's newspaper is unsaleable on Wednesday, and if one of the dozens of chapels perched at one or another of the numerous critical points in the production process chooses to be awkward, the newspaper's management has to decide whether to meet the chapel's demands or face losing an entire issue. The old proprietors generally paid up. Their motives – a mixture of vanity, political power-seeking and rivalry – compelled them to observe one priority above all: to publish. The unions' strong territorial instincts were matched by the proprietors', whose definition of territory was the share of the nation's newspaper readers they reached each day. Not to publish while their rivals did was something they could scarcely bear. But the habit of conceding remained even under the supposedly more tough-minded managements of the new corporations, and it was from years of conceding that the huge mountain range of excesses and inequities had sprung up which dominated Fleet Street and Times Newspapers.

If the newspaper proprietors had acted together through their own organisation, the NPA, they might have broken out of the long cycle of concessions. But the new owners were hardly more willing to demonstrate solidarity than the old proprietors had been. Schemes for common action had been discussed, one of which would have brought together all the other 'quality' newspapers – the *Guardian*, the *Telegraph*, the *Financial Times*, the *Observer* – at Times Newspapers, where they would all have been printed by a single, modern plant. But, characteristically, the owners could not agree. The nearest they came to success was in 1976, when the NPA negotiated a package of reforms with union leaders, only to have the package thrown out by a ballot of union members. After that disappointment there was little choice left but for each newspaper to go its own way. The Mirror Group had already struck out on its own, and now Times was going to do the same.

But for Times Newspapers to succeed with unions made extremely self-confident by the repeated success of their own aggressive tactics, its strategy would have to be very persuasive indeed. It would have to be either irresistibly attractive or irresistibly tough, or a very well-judged mixture of the two.

4
SILENT
SUMMER

The flurry of spring 1978 was followed by a strange lull. Hussey had written to the staff in April explaining how bad production was and promising action. Then in early May the *Guardian* leaked Hussey's letter to the general secretaries. Now we all knew about the November deadline. But after that we heard nothing except rumours on the grapevine, until in July the staff received a second letter from Hussey, which did little more than confirm some of the rumours. Meanwhile, tension mounted, and so did the toll of disputes and lost newspapers. It was bizarre. Hussey had told us there was a crisis which called for urgent action – but nothing whatever happened for months on end.

In this silence there began to take root among the staff a feeling which was to dog the company's entire strategy. It was a feeling that the company was not wholly serious, for if it had been, it would surely have followed up Hussey's April warning with speed. As it was, a full five months were to pass before anyone outside management learned details of the company's proposals. It was not until September that the staff began to discover for the first time exactly what it was supposed to do to avoid being sacked at the end of November. The delay seemed inexplicable, and all the blame for it fell on the company. More than a year was to pass before the management won back the credibility it lost in those silent months: it took from September 1978 to October of the next year for the company to convince the staff and their unions that it really did mean what it said.

Our picture of bland inactivity was misleading; the management was, in fact, extremely busy. Its shutdown strategy was in April no more than an outline, which now had to be filled in. Hussey's letter to the general secretaries only laid down broad aims, like peace, efficiency and higher wages. That was easily said; the difficulty lay in

converting the aims into detailed plans which could be put to the
dozens of chapels in Gray's Inn Road for negotiation. At the same
time the company had to keep the union leaders in step with its
thinking. Hussey's strategy depended on their giving his plans their
continuing consent. And that in turn depended on maintaining the
harmony that had seemed to exist at the April meetings. But the
harmony, such as it was, soon began to crumble.

The shifting mood was reflected in a letter sent by John Jackson of
Slade to Bill Keys of Sogat in July. Jackson wrote:

> I believe it is unfortunate that Mr Hussey and his other colleagues
> among the Times management seems to believe it is possible to reach
> an effective agreement or understanding with the union leaders over
> the heads of the chapels themselves or even in defiance of them. That
> may be contributing to the sense of conflict and suspicion affecting our
> members at the Times. Yet I know that if I suggest this to Mr Hussey
> he would read that as a lack of interest and enthusiasm in maintain-
> ing the stability and viability of the Times.

Jackson now wanted to 'involve our chapels and members in the
dialogue from the beginning' – a complete reversal of the negotiating
style which Hussey thought Jackson and the others had agreed.

An even more blunt reversal came from Joe Wade of the NGA. In
July his union's national council at last got around to considering
Hussey's April letter, and its response was a flat rejection. Wade's
reply to Hussey telling him so wore an air of injured innocence, of
how-could-you-do-this-to-me? Now, he claimed, the company's
plans were creating suspicion that it wanted 'to provoke a major confrontation with the unions'. And how that could be regarded as a
positive approach to problem-solving was now 'quite beyond comprehension'. If managements thought all they had to do to bring
unions to heel was to threaten to close a newspaper, then 'the sooner
that illusion is dispelled, the better for everyone in the national newspaper industry.' Wade's union had turned fastidious. Its officials at
any level – whether chapel father or general secretary – would not
discuss anything under threat of suspension or to a timetable with a
deadline at the end of it. Far from supporting Hussey, Wade now
wanted the company strategy aborted.

Unlike the NGA, the other unions did not refuse to meet the

company. But they did not actually come to a meeting either. Between 24 April and 18 September the union leaders did not meet the Times directors at all. This, it was said, was the company's fault, and so indignant did one union, Natsopa, become that in November it published its correspondence with the company to show that while it had been ready to talk all along, the company had only shilly-shallied.

Other correspondence files, however, reveal a fuller and a rather different picture. On 31 May Hussey wrote to tell Keys that by then only two unions had replied to his proposals, and that one of the two had suggested only that 'higher pay would resolve the outstanding issues'. Anxious to try to maintain the spirit of April, Hussey concluded: 'We will hold ourselves ready for a meeting at the earliest date convenient to you and your colleagues.'

Hussey's letter to Keys crossed in the post with a letter from Keys to Hussey, in which Keys said that his union's executive had endorsed the idea of joining with other unions to find solutions to the Times's problems. Once other unions had done the same, he said, 'We could consider a meeting between us.' Hussey welcomed that decision but, he told Keys, other unions had still not replied – the journalists, the electricians, the engineers and the NGA. Replies from those unions began to come in – the journalists' leader, Ken Ashton, wrote on 14 June and asked for another meeting without delay – but there was still silence from the NGA, a silence which was not broken for a further month, and then only by Wade's letter in which he refused to talk at all.

Keys, who throughout was to act as whipper-in on the union side, wrote again to Hussey on 31 July saying that both the NGA and Natsopa were creating difficulties about a meeting. He ended his letter despondently: 'I seem to be in check at the moment.' Ten days later the NGA confirmed its refusal to talk in a letter to Keys, and on the same day Hussey wrote to Keys in something near despair. The fact was, he said, that 'in spite of repeated requests the company has still been unable to arrange a meeting.'

There might, it seemed, be a chance of getting all the general secretaries together at Brighton in the first week of September, where they would be gathered for the annual Congress of the TUC. Keys told his branches towards the end of August that he was 'trying des-

perately hard' to arrange it. But he failed. This time it was Owen
O'Brien of Natsopa who rang Hussey's office to say that TUC week
would not be convenient.

On 14 September the Times executive board met to settle the final
details of the negotiating plan it would put to the union general secretaries at a meeting which had been pencilled in for the 18th. Two
days earlier Hussey and Nisbet-Smith had travelled up from London
to the NGA's headquarters in Bedford to try once more to persuade
that union to reconsider its refusal to talk to the company at all. They
had found Les Dixon and Joe Wade wavering but non-committal.

But now Hussey was summoned out of the board meeting to take
a call from Wade. Yes, Wade said, he would come on the 18th, but
only on condition that the company did not raise the question of new
technology. Hussey agreed. At long last a meeting with the general
secretaries could be firmly inked into diaries. Five months after the
directors had got, or thought they had got, the approval of the union
leaders for their shutdown strategy they were at last to meet them
again.

The company had been ready to open serious negotiations in July,
but its strategy required it to begin with the general secretaries, and
it was unable to arrange a meeting with them until September. Four
of the seven months between April and November were wasted, and
the unions were at least partly to blame. In the mythology of the
dispute, however, it was all the company's fault.

Part of the delay for which the company was responsible had been
caused by the difficulty management had in coming up with detailed
proposals to fill out Hussey's grand strategy. For what the company
wanted from its managers was no less radical than what it wanted
from the staff and the unions. Managers were asked to rethink completely the operations of their departments. But their habits of mind
were as ingrained and conservative as those of the staff they super-
vised – not surprisingly, since all but the most senior management
was promoted from the shop floor. Supervisors belonged to the same
unions as their staffs, if only because some unions would not allow
their members to take orders from people who were not also union
members. One manager, asked to rethink his operations, promptly
demanded a rise in salary. 'Rethinking' was extra work and extra
work meant extra money – at least, it had when he was an ordinary

employee. Next day he was told that he would get more money, but in the form of a golden handshake. He was fired for not behaving as an employer should.

While the union leaders stayed away the company's detailed proposals – known as New Agreement Proposals or NAPs – were held on ice, and over the summer months only one item of its plans was released: a new disputes procedure, which Hussey sent to the general secretaries in a confidential letter in July. The proposed procedure was highly ambitious. It laid down that if any chapel became involved in a dispute that stopped production, the whole staff would have to go unpaid until the dispute was ended. That would have meant that the pay cheques of every chapel would be vulnerable to action taken by any one of more than sixty other chapels. This was how things were done in Canada and Hussey's plan fitted in with the thinking of the Toronto office. But it is not how things are done in Britain, where unions strenuously avoid any such penalty clauses. Hussey thought it was worth trying all the same. If he put something forward that was tough, the unions might respond with something less tough but perhaps workable. His letter was cautiously phrased to encourage the union leaders not to reject it flat but to come back with ideas of their own. But the unions' response was disappointing, and Hussey's tactic did not get far.

There was another problem which the company found hard to think through. It had presented the staff with a threat to dismiss every employee if the company did not get the agreements it wanted from the unions by 30 November; but how was management to exercise its threat? The simplest option might have been to lock out the whole staff on the deadline date. Overnight that would have thrown more than 4000 people on the unions to support, which would have enormously increased the pressure on the unions to settle quickly.

But a lockout had dangers too, and recent experiences of that kind of employer aggression had been discouraging. At Grunwick, a photo-processing company in north London, staff who went on strike had been fired, and the result was thousands of pickets fighting thousands of policemen in the streets day after day. Times Newspapers had no wish to turn Gray's Inn Road into another battlefield. Besides, a lockout might so sicken the creative staff, especially the journalists and the marketing department, that they would simply leave, and the best would have been the first to find other jobs. To Brunton and the Times board the assets of the newspapers were little more than the sum of the talents of those departments, and their collapse would be disastrous.

So the management leaned towards a gentler tactic, though it was one that was more confusing and led the company into a legal nightmare. It would fire only staff whose unions failed to make agreements by the deadline, and it would not dismiss them on the spot but would let them serve out their notice. With luck, that would ensure that the journalists were never in danger of losing their jobs and it would also, it was hoped, show the management to be moderate and reasonable.

More moderate this tactic may have been, but letting staff serve out their notice could mean that the company would keep more than half its work force on full pay for three months, which would severely reduce the pressure on the unions. And the legality of the tactic was dangerously uncertain. If it came to a court case, the company intended to argue that it had offered the staff reasonable terms of employment, so it was fair to dismiss those who had refused to accept the terms. But the courts might rule that the action was unfair, or they might hold that it constituted not dismissal at all but redundancy. Either judgement would cost the company a very great deal in compensation.

In order to keep its options open and its liabilities down, the company had to dress its policy in highly obscure lawyer's language, as in this notice, filed formally with the Government and leaked in the *Daily Telegraph*: 'In certain circumstances on or after November 30, the company may dismiss all or some of its employees. All or some of these dismissals may be for redundancy.' This kind of legal gobbledegook baffled the staff, who could not discover what it meant for them, and much time was to be spent on arguing about that instead of on negotiating the company's proposals.

The board finally settled its tactics on 14 September: it would only give notice, and only to those who had not settled with it. Harold Evans tried to get the deadline postponed. He had not been closely involved in the company's planning since April, and the scale of its ambitions was only now beginning to dawn on him. The company, he thought, was asking the staff to digest too much in too little time. Another director, Donald Cruickshank, sympathised with Evans's worries; time, he acknowledged, could be the company's Achilles' heel. But Evans found no support for postponing the deadline. The company was too heavily committed to 30 November for the Thomson Organisation to let it draw back.

Hussey had fixed the meeting on the 18th for the Russell Hotel, not far away in Bloomsbury, a regular sanctuary for discreet union negotiations in many industries over the years. But television and the rest of the press were beginning to take a serious interest in the Times affairs. The day after the executive board meeting the *Daily Telegraph* carried a story that could have been taken to mean that Times Newspapers intended to fire all its staff, and practically forthwith. Two union general secretaries immediately called Hussey to protest. Hussey reassured them that that was not what he planned to do. But he was anxious for his meeting with the general secretaries to take place without that sort of publicity, so he made a last-minute switch to the Bristol Hotel in Mayfair. There was an irony about a newspaper company's attempt to hide from the press, and Times directors were to be intermittently self-conscious about this throughout the dispute. In any case, they failed on this occasion and many later ones. Reporters and cameramen were at the Bristol to catch the union leaders when they left.

What Hussey wanted from the general secretaries was their go-ahead for the intensive phase of negotiations on the NAPs to begin; what he got was a lukewarm assent which was far from encouraging. The spirit of April had totally vanished. With the deadline only two and a half months away, the union leaders began to take refuge in the issue of delays. Bill Keys and Owen O'Brien both made a special point of it. Both told reporters that they had been ready to negotiate since May. 'Nothing has happened since then,' Keys said. 'Everything has suddenly crystallised today.' They would not prevent the negotiations from starting, though – unlike Joe Wade, who did. He now reverted to the NGA's July position, from which he had moved only far enough to attend the meeting. The NGA would talk again if the company withdrew its threat of closure, but not otherwise.

With that meeting, the first long round of shadow-boxing ended. Negotiations proper began, and the first real test of the company's strategy got under way. The omens were poor. Delay had embittered the staff and made it suspicious, and the ambiguities over what might happen to it – who might be fired and how – soured the mood further. The first sight of the NAPs which now began to trickle out dismayed many people, even the journalists. One union, the NGA, was not willing to negotiate at all, and the leaders of the other unions were hardly enthusiastic. It would take prodigious skill and a great deal of luck for the newspapers to survive the deadline.

5
TIMES
LOST

The detailed proposals for change which the company put to the chapels under the title of NAPs were like prisms. What you saw in them depended very much on your angle of vision.

Looked at one way, they were moderation itself. Times Newspapers was part of a nineteenth-century industry that needed to be brought up to date. It was just like coal, steel, shipbuilding, the railways and the ports. All of these had had to come to terms with the modern world at one time or another over the previous twenty years, and by their standards the Times medicine was mild stuff. Like the other industries, the Times wanted to lose staff – 22 per cent overall – but, unlike them, it was not proposing to force people to leave. Nobody would be compelled to go if he did not want to. Those who went would get generous pay-offs; natural attrition would take care of others; while those who stayed would get higher pay. To a steelworker in the late 1970s, the Times prescription would have seemed heaven-sent.

But there were other ways of looking at the NAPs. Fleet Street was not subject to the same annihilating competition as those other industries – coal from oil, or rail from roads. If other newspapers could make do with the traditional methods, the Times should stick to them too. The way in which the company was trying to break out of old patterns cut straight through deeply entrenched rights and interests. New technology was the most obvious case. But the underlying drift of the NAPs, with their implicit reassertion of managerial authority over union power, was just as hard for many people to accept.

Ramshackle and anarchic the union system undoubtedly was, but at a time when social relations of all kinds were becoming looser and more egalitarian and when industrial democracy was enjoying a pronounced political vogue, it was in one respect at least extremely modern. It gave workers a high degree of control. No boss pushed anybody about; the chapels saw to that.

Here, perhaps more than anywhere else in British industry, management had to be conducted with the consent of the managed. In Fleet Street equality of a kind had been achieved. It was rough and ready, more a dangerously unstable truce between two armed camps than a Utopia of mutual co-operation. But it was real enough all the same. Thrust into this context, the NAPs jarred. They seemed to be a step back into a more authoritarian past. Nor was this only the reaction of a few militants. Even the journalists were shocked when they saw the NAPs the company had prepared for them.

It had never occurred to me to compare Harold Evans with Napoleon. The comparison did, however, occur to John Barry, the father of the *Sunday Times*'s journalists' chapel, after he had made a careful study of the NAP which was delivered to us at the end of October.

From Barry's reading Evans emerged looking like the Napoleon rendered by the artist David, heroically crossing the Alps at the head of his army: 'the benevolent despot astride his flaming white charger, while his devoted infantry trudge mutely after'. According to this image, we journalists were the poor bloody infantry in the service of Evans the despot. Journalism, the NAP seemed to say, was henceforth to be whatever Evans said it was. He could invite anybody he ever he wanted, no matter what the views of the owner, the management, the journalists, the unions or anybody else; and he could publish whatliked to fill any amount of space in the paper; he could forbid his journalists to write or broadcast for other people. Evans was to be the sovereign of a newspaper empire; in him alone was to be invested the ideals of press freedom, as the ideals of the French Revolution had become invested in the Emperor Napoleon.

'Why', Barry somewhat whimsically inquired in the long analysis he wrote of our NAP, 'should a *Sunday Times* journalist who, in private life, translates Greek verse, have to get the editor's permission to discuss Greek verse on television?' To Barry, one series of clauses in the NAP was 'symptomatic of the evident desire of the management to treat journalists as assembly-line serfs rather than reasonable staff', while another series seemed to 'vest total rights in the editor but impose no corresponding duties upon him – precisely the combination of ills most criticised by the *Sunday Times* when evidenced by the unions'.

This was strong stuff, even allowing for the eye-catching style which Barry had developed over the years as writer of many of the *Sunday Times*'s most arresting inquiries. Barry was no chapel militant. He was one of Evans's longest-serving and most senior executives, so senior that there had been an undercurrent of disquiet among the journalists about the fact that he had been elected chapel father.

But if Barry's reaction was overblown, so was my own. I was so angry at the diminished place in the world to which our NAP assigned us that I rang the editor of the *Spectator*, Alexander Chancellor, and asked if he would publish something by me about it. It was not that I was bursting to say anything in particular; I just wanted to prove that I could still write without asking anybody's permission.

Chancellor agreed. When I mentioned to Evans that I was writing the piece he frowned momentarily, but then he said: 'Oh, well . . . freedom of the press . . . I can't stop you.' And when it was published he told me he agreed with most of its complaints about the lowered status of journalists implied by the company's proposals. Not surprisingly, I was confused. Did Evans agree with the journalists' NAP? And if he did, could he also agree with my article? Barry summed up his confusion and my own: 'the management – for reasons which are baffling – seeks to change the whole atmosphere on the *Sunday Times* from one of co-operation to one of "discipline".'

In fact, neither the company nor Evans wanted to change its relations with the journalists. The confusion stemmed from the style of the NAPs, all of which were couched in the same prescriptive language. This was deliberate: the company was anxious not to be seen talking to different chapels in different tones of voice. For most chapels the result was an exhaustive list of all the things their members were expected to do for their pay. By defining everybody's job in fine detail, nothing would be left to argue about. Argument only led to negotiation and negotiation to disputes – which was exactly what the company was trying to stop.

The journalists' NAP was subtly different from the others. It did not try to define our work (wisely, for what a journalist actually does for a living – a strange amalgam of action and inaction, luxury and squalor, reading, gossiping, making notes and writing it all down – defies precise definition). But a discordant, authoritarian note contrived to find its way into our NAP all the same. It arose, paradoxically, from Evans's concern with press freedom. To him it was a delicate plant, most likely to be maintained in good health if put under the care of one person – the editor of the newspaper, himself. His concern was shared by the journalists; but, translated into the stiff, unbending terms of an NAP, it became offensive. The NAPs had that way with them. They made acceptable aims unacceptable.

NAPS were not, however, carved in tablets of stone. Insensitive though they were, it was still up to each chapel to decide how to respond. Each could boggle and protest or sit down around the table with management negotiators in one of the rooms in the executive suite on the seventh floor of New Printing House Square and pare away at the bits of the company's proposals it did not like.

The journalists decided to negotiate. It took the *Sunday Times* chapel just over a month of endless meetings – meetings between members of the chapel committee, with the management and with the rest of the journalists – hacking away at the NAP until it was carved to an acceptable shape. We were held up mainly over questions that turned out not to matter, like how much we would be paid if the company folded. It took up a lot of time and it was extremely boring. All we had done in a month was to return more or less to where we had started. We were to be £500 a year better off, but we could write elsewhere and broadcast as freely as ever, if not more freely, and in every other detail that mattered life at the *Sunday Times* would be for us just what it had always been. On 28 November the chapel voted to accept the NAP.

It was a tribute to the clumsiness of the NAPs that the *Sunday Times* journalists (who had no quarrel with the company, nor it with us) should have taken so long to reach agreement. If we could find ourselves in such a tangle, what might happen with other unions and others chapels which were separated from the company by issues of real substance?

Of all the issues, new technology was by far the most sensitive. Just how sensitive I discovered in November, when I wrote for the *Sunday Times* an assessment of the state of play in the negotiations.

Late on Saturday afternoon Frank Giles, the deputy editor who was in charge of the paper while Evans was away, called me to his office. He had, a few minutes before, received a deputation from the NGA. In the friendliest possible way he had been told that the NGA would not handle the page in which my article was to appear unless the wording was changed. Without the page the *Sunday Times* could not be published. Giles therefore agreed to make alterations. There was no time left for rewriting before the first edition went to press, so the article was 'hammered'. The offending words were chipped out of the metal plates which printed that page, creating an odd-looking, fuzzy hole in the published newspaper and an equally fuzzy gap in the logic of the article.

It was a quote from the NGA's most senior chapel father, John Carey, that had provoked the deputation. I had quoted Carey as saying, in connection with the question of who should operate the new typesetting keyboards, 'I think a compromise position could be reached.' I was sure the quote was accurate, and Carey displayed the same attitude, though in slightly different words, two days later on television. But the deputation was in no mood to hear a defence. The message of its appearance in Giles's office was that a compromise on keystroking was not possible. It was a striking demonstration of the union's feelings. If the journalists disliked the threat to their freedoms contained in the company's proposals, the NGA disliked the company's plans for single keystroking infinitely more.

The electronic system which Times Newspapers had bought and made ready would take the company in one bound from the late nineteenth to the late twentieth century. It had been discovered several years before by Roy Thomson, who found it in operation at a small newspaper he had bought in Los Angeles, the San Gabriel Valley *Tribune*. Full of enthusiasm, Thomson had called Hussey and told him it was exactly what the Times needed. Mander was about to leave for California, and Hussey asked him to look at the newspaper while he was there. Mander did, and was caught with the same enthusiasm. He rang Hussey from Los Angeles, getting Hussey up from the breakfast table, to tell him that he had already made an appointment to see the system's Californian inventors, Systems Development Corporation (SDC). Other companies were later invited to tender, but it was the SDC system which the Times eventually bought.

From the company's point of view, the system had more than one advantage. It could be tied in with the commercial side of the newspaper's business, so that computers could run instant credit checks on advertisers, for whom they would also automatically spew out a bill. This function of the system seems to have aroused Thomson's greatest enthusiasm. It was the other, typesetting, function that aroused the NGA's opposition. For the computers would also let tele-ad girls and journalists prepare their material in a form that would by-pass the NGA operators in the composing room.

Elsewhere in the industralised world, and especially in America, newspapers had approached the electronic era earlier, but in stages. They had first adapted the Linotype to run automatically, fed by punched tape. Then they abandoned the Linotype and hot metal for 'cold type'. But in those first two stages the keyboards which punched the tape or set the 'cold type' were still worked by operators, not journalists. Only with the arrival of computers was it possible for journalists to perform two functions at once – to write their stories and set them in type – with a single keystroke. And it was only after considerable experience of the first two stages that American newspapers had gone on to the third.

By installing the SDC system, the Times was proposing to go to stage three virtually in one leap. This was a bold manoeuvre to attempt in the face of a powerful union with important interests to protect. The company had done something to prepare the way, however. In 1976 it had circulated the staff with a pamphlet describing the new equipment, and it had also gone through its plan with the leaders of all the print unions, both individually and together at a dinner. But it had not consulted the unions in advance about the kind of equipment it intended to use. Only after it had made up its own mind did the company turn its attention to persuading the staff and the unions.

In the circumstances, this was an inherently risky procedure, all the more so since the NGA had turned down another newspaper group with similar technological ambitions, the Portsmouth and Sunderland, even while the Times was installing its new computers on the third floor of the *Sunday Times* building, where they had immediately become objects of suspicion and symbols of menace. The NGA's decision to refuse the Portsmouth and Sunderland group was to form the basis of its policy towards all new electronic systems. It would accept them only if they were worked 'back-end' by NGA members, not 'front-end' by journalists. But the Times system was specifically designed to work 'front-end'.

In the company's thinking, it would have made little difference to the job prospects of NGA members whether the new systems were operated front- or back-end, at any rate in the short term. It intended to phase in the equipment, starting with the *Times Literary Supplement* in 1979 and gradually spreading it through the other publications. Worked entirely back-end, a cut of almost half the number of NGA jobs would still be needed because the electronic keyboards created type far faster than Linotypes. But the computer age was developing quickly. Systems were out of date almost before they were ready to be used. It was not difficult for the NGA to imagine that once it had agreed to single keystroking, on no matter how limited a scale, it would have sold the pass. One thing would lead to another. Computers would multiply and keyboards proliferate, and the union and its members would be driven out of the industry within a few years. The key to the future seemed to lie in control of the keyboard, and the NGA was determined to retain its ancient monopoly. Keystroking thus became an issue of bedrock principle for the union.

The company was fully aware of the delicacy of the issue. At a series of meetings in the early months of 1978 – three in March, two in April, one each in May, June and July – it had established a good deal of preliminary common ground with the NGA. The union agreed to shift from hot metal to 'cold type'. It would give up the London piece-rate system which generated earnings for a few that were the envy of the whole British union movement. It would merge the composing rooms of the *Times* and the *Sunday Times* and accept a cut of almost half in the number of jobs. But so far the negotiations had skirted round the question of keyboarding.

To the Times board this was a question of a different order from those issues of disruption and inefficiency which had led it to opt for the shutdown strategy. The NGA compositors were for the most part neither disruptive nor inefficient, and while their negotiators were still talking to the company in the first half of the year, it seemed sensible to keep the new technology separate from the package of issues which the company wanted to settle before the November deadline.

But when, in July, the NGA decided not to talk at all as long as the deadline remained, it made increasingly less sense to treat technology separately. Time was running out on the company's plan to start using 'cold type' in 1979. Kenneth Thomson was extremely keen that the new system should be used to the full, as it was in his North American newspapers. Keystroking was an issue sensitive enough to be the cause of confrontation on its own. Why risk closing the newspaper twice? In September, therefore, the board agreed to include keystroking in its deadline package.

That decision was, however, less than conclusive. Throughout, the company was to be ambivalent in its tactics, almost to the point of confusion. Two weeks before the September board meeting Mander had asked Hussey in a memo: 'Is new technology included in November 30th or not?' Even after the board meeting, management at the highest level was not sure where things stood. As late as 1 November Gordon Brunton sent a secret memo to Hussey which contained a series of questions about how the Times was handling its negotiations. One paragraph revealed his uncertainty: 'What are the real objectives that you are seeking to achieve?' Brunton asked.

> My colleagues and I understood that those objectives were limited ones relating to continuity of production, new disputes procedures and an agreement to examine manning levels based upon voluntary redundancies. What I am not clear about is whether one of the conditions also relates to the introduction of new technology and, indeed, I believe this may be a 'grey area' in the thinking of you and your colleagues.

Brunton was right. Keystroking was a grey area in the company's thinking, over which it was to change its mind more than once.

The NGA, too, changed its mind, or seemed to. In July, it decided not to talk while the deadline remained. In September, Wade emerged from the shelter of that decision to meet the company with the other general secretaries, on condition that new technology was not discussed. He left that meeting committed not to talk again until the company lifted its deadline. But the union soon changed tack once more. It would talk, but only about new technology and only if the company agreed not to make deals on its use with other unions behind the NGA's back. Hussey agreed, and a meeting was set up for 10 November in the boardroom of New Printing House Square.

Nisbet-Smith opened the meeting by saying he was ready to talk all day. He had laid on a buffet lunch so that nobody need leave the office. But Les Dixon, who was to lead the NGA negotiators throughout most of the rest of the dispute, was not in a conciliatory mood. Having already seen the proposals on new technology the company had put to the journalists, he made it bluntly clear that he did not like what he saw. Though the journalists were not being asked to take on single keystroking unless the NGA agreed, they were being asked to commit themselves to the principle of it, and it was this principle the NGA was committed to oppose. Dixon therefore asked the company to rewrite completely its operational plans for the new technology.

Though disappointed with Dixon's rigidity, Nisbet-Smith was not surprised. He had come prepared. 'Why not take this off the table?' he asked Dixon. Let the NGA agree the rest of the company's proposals and keystroking could be deferred until after the deadline for discussion between the NGA's national council and the Times board. Dixon, interested, asked to see Nisbet-Smith's latest proposal in writing. The meeting adjourned shortly before noon, and Dixon took away a carefully constructed three-paragraph letter which Nisbet-Smith and Hussey, expecting the worst, had prepared beforehand.

Over lunch Dixon and his team studied the letter. The first two paragraphs looked all right. They excluded single keystroking from the deadline and promised it would not happen at all without the NGA's agreement. The sting lay in the third paragraph, which said that discussion must begin on the 'principle and practice of keystroking'. This implied that there was something left to discuss. It would keep single keystroking firmly on the agenda, whereas the NGA wanted it removed from the agenda altogether. Accepting Nisbet-Smith's letter would leave open a door which the NGA was determined to keep shut. Before the end of the afternoon Dixon had rejected the letter, and a week later his stand was endorsed by the NGA national council.

The company made one final effort to propitiate the NGA's fears. A few days after the abortive meeting Nisbet-Smith wrote to Dixon to make it clear that front-ending would not cost the NGA any more jobs than it had already shown a willingness to lose as part of the switch from hot metal to 'cold type'. No matter how much keyboarding journalists and others might do, the company would keep the same number of NGA men on its payroll. In his letter Nisbet-Smith offered to fix the numbers for five years; in private he was ready to go to ten.

But the NGA was not disposed to haggle. Its leaders now saw keystroking in terms that were little short of apocalyptic. Wade wrote to Hussey that the ramifications of conceding would be 'catastrophic', and that his national council was 'determined to fight this issue to the bitter end'. A few days before the deadline Wade wrote in his union journal a warning that was also a call to arms:

> In industrial life, as elsewhere, there are some battles you win and some you lose – and if you lose a battle, it doesn't necessarily mean that you have lost the war. But the outcome of the war over new technology will now be determined by the battle at the Times – of that I am sure. So there is no going back. There can be no surrender. We fight for our members. We fight for our union. We fight until we have won.

For the NGA everything had now become unambiguously focused on one issue: keyboarding. Other questions were negotiable, but the union would not discuss the single keystroke, before or after the deadline. The company seemed equally insistent: the NGA must concede, if not before the deadline, then later. Yet, strangely, in spite of the obvious commitment of both sides, neither could quite believe the other meant what it said. In private, senior men from the union and the company often told me they did not think keystroking was the real problem. It seemed absurd to the NGA that the management should insist when the union had already made so many concessions to the new technology, especially over jobs. But to the management it seemed perverse of the NGA to jib at the last half-inch when it had conceded most of a mile.

Company and union were, however, increasingly trapped in the postures which they had adopted. The company had been willing to take keystroking out of the immediate agenda, providing that the NGA would agree to talk about it later. But when the NGA refused the company's attitude hardened. Meanwhile, the spectacle of the NGA and the Times so obviously at loggerheads had its effect on other unions, which saw no reason for rushing to make settlements of their own. Without the NGA the newspapers would lose anyway. Materially, measured by jobs and money, single keystroking might not be very important; psychologically, it was crucial. In the shadow cast by the deadlock over that issue, other unions bided their time.

Management and union officials who said that the real problem at Times Newspapers was not new technology knew perfectly well where they thought the problem lay – not in departments overwhelmed by new methods, but among some regular and some casual staff in clerical work and the machine room, where, to the outside eye, the changes the company wanted were not remarkable. If pressed, officials were willing to be more specific and to identify as the toughest nuts for the company to crack two individuals, Barry Fitzpatrick and Reg Brady, both fathers of *Sunday Times* Natsopa chapels, Fitzpatrick of the clerks and Brady of the machine room.

Brady was a child of the print trade; his father and grandfather had been in it before him. As a boy he had played on the wooden chutes down which newspapers dropped on to waiting lorries at the old Kemsley House, and he had started work as a printer's devil at fourteen, becoming a brake hand and working regular shifts at the *Evening Standard* and *Reveille* as well as Saturday nights at the *Sunday Times*. Now in his mid-forties, he cut something of a dandified figure, with his greying hair in waves, his narrow beard wrapped close around his chin and his taste for snappy dressing. There was a touch of the showman too in his negotiating style. He liked to present an out-size image of himself, whether of extreme reasonableness or of militancy. Managers who negotiated with him could never be quite sure how to read him. If he rejected something out of hand, in a welter of adjectives, did he mean what he said or was he putting it on? His opposite numbers usually found it wise to assume the worst.

Fitzpatrick, a decade younger, was cast in an altogether less flamboyant mould. Serious, dogged, persistent, he seemed willing to spend infinities of time and patience in negotiation, examining every detail of any new proposal, turning it this way and that in the search for flaws, checking and rechecking the meaning of each phrase. So much time would he take that it came to seem to the company like a tactic in itself, less blunt and more sophisticated than Brady's outspokenness perhaps, but no less effective a brake on agreement.

But these two very different men had at least one thing in common. Both had shown signs of high ambition. Brady was not only a chapel father at the *Sunday Times* but had held office at the *Evening Standard* too. For four years in the 1960s he had been a full-time official of Natsopa. He had even gone so far as to apply for a job on the other side, with the employers, as nothing less than director of the NPA. His application led to an interview during which he was asked what he thought was the most important problem in Fleet Street. His reply was astonishingly candid; over-manning in the machine rooms. One of his interviewers was Lord Goodman, chairman of the *Observer* and of the NPA. The other was Hussey. Brady did not become the NPA director. But his interview must have left an ominous memory with Hussey, whose demands on Brady's machine room chapel included a large reduction in manning.

Fitzpatrick too was more than a chapel father at the *Sunday Times*. He was chairman of the union's London clerical branch and, like Brady, a member of its national executive. He and Brady had also done something in 1978 that was perhaps even more unconventional than Brady's bid for the NPA directorship. They had both challenged Owen O'Brien for the leadership of Natsopa.

Union rules laid down that the general secretary be subject to reelection, but in living memory there had never actually been a contest while the incumbent wanted to stay. It was simply not done to challenge the holder of the office before he reached retirement. Now both Brady and Fitzpatrick had presented themselves as candidates.

Brady, however, did not get far. He failed to get on to the ballot paper. O'Brien's predecessor, Richard Briginshaw, had devised a test, a quirky oral examination, which would-be general secretaries had to pass before they could stand for election. It was more a memory test than a searching intellectual inquiry, but Fitzpatrick passed and Brady did not. Fitzpatrick went on to run up a respectable score of votes against O'Brien, though not enough to win. Later he and Brady stood again, this time against Teddy O'Brien, Owen's brother, who was one of the union's three assistant general secretaries. Again, neither won against the sitting official. And Brady was to fail for a third time when he ran for the union presidency.

These failures of Brady and Fitzpatrick were less significant than the fact of their challenge to the union's leaders. It underlined the fact that authority in Natsopa was in an exceptionally uncertain state. There was, besides, a whiff of scandal in the air, released by a group of activist members centred on the *Observer*, who had exercised their right to look at the union's books and had begun to come up with some bizarre findings – mysterious property transactions, Swiss bank accounts, loans to private companies of which union officers were also directors. Nobody suggested that Owen O'Brien himself was involved in any of these things, but he had been a senior official when they happened, and the discoveries inevitably put his regime on the defensive.

In this uneasy atmosphere the row at Times Newspapers presented a rare opportunity to rank-and-file leaders with ambition. A union's top leadership generally controls most of the sources of power in the union, especially its lines of communication. It is the top man's name that appears on the union notepaper; his photograph is generously displayed in the union journal; and he, if anybody, is quoted in newspapers and broadcasts. A well-publicised dispute is one of the few ways in which a junior rival may break out of the obscurity which usually smothers him. And the Times dispute was nothing if not well-publicised.

But whatever opportunities the dispute might throw up for ambitious chapel fathers, the company's plans were a direct challenge to the power they already held. This was, indeed, the underlying theme of the Times strategy. The company had set out deliberately to reduce the power of the fathers and increase the power of its own managers, with, it believed, the support of the staff's own union leaders and that of the whole trade union establishment. But the plans represented a challenge to the fathers, and they did not fail to rise to it.

The nature of chapel power varied. In the case of Brady's 540-strong chapel it arose from the casual system under which all his members worked. In theory, casual work was a convenience to management. Newspapers could turn the supply of men on and off, like water from a tap, according to need. The *Sunday Times* did not have to employ full time all the men it needed for its huge production run on one night of the week, Saturday. Over the years, however, the practice had moved a long way from the theory. It was the union's hand that controlled the tap. Newspapers hired men through their union. The union call office sent the men round, and the chapel officer allocated them their jobs, their shifts, their time off – called 'blows' – and their holidays. In all but name, managerial power in casual departments had been ceded to the unions.

Casual work gave unions another source of power. Because casual workers had jobs at more than one newspaper, they did not rely on one employer to pay all their wages. Provided employment held up in Fleet Street as a whole, casual workers could remain detached about what happened at any one newspaper house. If one newspaper failed, they could always make up their pay elsewhere.

At the best of times Fleet Street was highly vulnerable to chapel pressure, and in the interests of peace and production it had regularly given in. As a result, a series of exotic practices had grown up, not least among casual chapels, which were known affectionately as 'old Spanish customs'. The *Sunday Times* was contracted to pay 540 wage packets to Brady's chapel every Saturday night. But did 540 men all work a full shift every Saturday night, or did that number even turn up for work? So far had management let control slip to the union that it simply did not know, though it had well-grounded suspicions. The company paid out 540 wage packets for sure, but some were drawn by men with strange names like 'M. Mouse of Sunset Boulevard, Hollywood' or even 'Marmaduke Hussey' himself. Could it be that some men were drawing two wage packets? That was what the company believed, and so did the Inland Revenue, which had begun to take a close interest in the earnings of Mickey

Mouse and his friends. (One Inland Revenue survey was to show that in a sample of Fleet Street casual workers' pay packets more than 50 per cent were drawn under false names.)

The company's proposals would undermine the casual system at several points. The union would still supply the labour but the company would manage it. 135 jobs would be cut from the 540 of Brady's chapel. But because the company would oversee its work force, there would actually be more real shifts worked than before. The changes would radically reduce the managerial power of the chapel and of its father, Brady. And the cut in jobs would reduce the pool of work available to all the members of the union's London machine branch, of which the *Sunday Times* chapel was a part. The proposals threatened all these linked interests – Brady, the chapel, the branch and the branch members – and if Brady himself were inclined to resist, he could expect many supporters.

The nature of power in Fitzpatrick's clerical chapel was quite different from that of Brady's. Being regular employees and not casuals, his members did not have the strength conferred by easy withdrawal that Brady's did. But they had something else. They had caught the Fleet Street habit of constant negotiation.

To someone unused to an intensely unionised industry like Fleet Street, this habit may seem outlandish. Surely, he will think, a union makes regular pay claims, say once a year, and deals with odd problems in between times, but that is about all. That was the way some unions, like the journalists', played the game, but it was not the only way to play it. There was nothing to stop a chapel from turning every least act or decision of management into an issue to argue or negotiate over. It paid off in hard cash, but money was not the only motive. Journalists were no less eager to be well paid than anybody else, yet their union did not go in for ceaseless bargaining. The difference is not easy to account for. Probably it is a mixture of satisfaction in work, attitudes to trade unionism, scope for individual action, temperament and personalities. What is clear is that if it wants to, a chapel can develop its power to the point at which it matches and even merges with the power of management, so that nobody is any longer quite sure what his role is or who is in charge.

One independent account of this world of disputed rights exists in the form of a lengthy judgement by an industrial tribunal on a claim for unfair dismissal by four members of the *Sunday Times* clerical chapel. The dismissals happened after the newspaper was shut. The staff was slimming down as notices ran out, but the chapel had decided that those who were left should not cover the work of those who had gone. The four men, short-credit clerks who handled advertisement accounts and whose notices had not yet expired, refused to do the job of a fifth clerk in the same department who had already gone. They went to the tribunal to claim that their dismissal was unfair because it is unlawful to dismiss anybody for trade union activities.

But what is a trade union activity? And what are the rights of employers and employees? Evidently, the management was not sure where it stood. As Mrs Stella Hollis, the tribunal chairman, wrote in her judgement:

> It is quite clear that the management throughout felt themselves on very sticky ground indeed. They had gone to the length of having a barrister in attendance before they made what was really a perfectly straightforward management decision. In the circumstances existing management functions had become so eroded that the managers no longer recognised with confidence what was a proper management decision to take and what was not. They felt they had to have a barrister around to advise them whether they could legitimately ask one clerk to do another clerk's job.

The chapel did not share the management's uncertainties. Fitzpatrick gave evidence to the tribunal, on which Mrs Hollis commented:

> Having seen Mr Fitzpatrick I am quite satisfied that he is a reasonable and sensible man and that under normal circumstances and indeed throughout this unpleasant interlude he probably did have good relationships face to face with the management. He himself however has been caught up in practices which have been referred to in the course of this hearing as 'old Spanish customs'. Some of the 'old Spanish customs' have been relied upon by the applicants as a contractual addendum to their contracts of employment. The particular relevant old Spanish custom being that where there is any change which seems to affect or in any way impinge upon the work of one of the employees, however minimal and however in ordinary circumstances it could not be regarded as change either in their con-

tract or in their normal conditions of employment, then that change would have to be discussed with and accepted by the trade union before that change however minimal it may be can be enforced by management.

To Mrs Hollis this was a novel proposition and, being novel, it required backing. But, she went on:

There has not been produced before me any evidence to suggest that this practice is other than one which over the years has grown and grown. It certainly seems to me that the 'old Spanish customs' were something which might just as well have been referred to as inherited myths of somewhat dubious parentage. They are certainly myths that Mr Fitzpatrick inherited, deeply believes in and may have affected absolutely everything that took place.

Mrs Hollis took the view that management was fully entitled to ask the four clerks to do the work of the fifth. But that left another question. Were the four entitled to refuse, on the grounds that by doing so they were 'taking part at an appropriate time in a trade union activity'? On this Mrs Hollis was firm:

It seems to me that to suggest that they were makes a nonsense of the English language. It seems to me that a trade union activity is a constructive thing. It seems to me that a trade union activity has to relate to an end product of the trade union. The words 'appropriate time' suggest a non-continuing act, quite different from that which occurred here. It does not seem to me that what they were doing amounted to a trade union activity.

The clerks lost their argument. But the judgement of their case was deeply revealing of the attitudes in Gray's Inn Road. Power of the kind claimed by the clerks' chapel may have had no basis in law or in normal industrial practice, but the notion that it was valid all the same had a strong grip on the minds of those who worked at the Times, managers no less than trade unionists. No matter what the law might say, chapel power was a reality and it was not likely to be given up lightly.

Well before the NAPs were given out in October the Natsopa chapel fathers sensed the way things were going. No sooner had Hussey's letter to the general secretaries setting out the shutdown strategy leaked in early May than Reg Brady wrote to Hussey objecting in the strongest possible terms to the threat of a lockout. In July he wrote again, complaining that Hussey had broken the law by declining to reveal information about the company's plans to him, the authorised union negotiator, and threatening to take legal advice or even to report Hussey to the Government. Later the same month eleven Natsopa fathers addressed a collective letter to Hussey saying they would not negotiate at all under a deadline threat and insisting that negotiations must be with them, not their union's leaders. Hussey replied in soothing terms, but the fathers were not persuaded. They realised that Hussey's aim was to cut them down in size by bringing the weight of their union leaders to bear on negotiations that would undermine their authority.

Owen O'Brien had difficulty in getting his union to the negotiating table. At the end of September, immediately after he had agreed to negotiate in the way the company wanted – with union officials there to keep a check on the chapel fathers – the fathers fired off a telegram to the company refusing to negotiate at all under duress. A few days later, however, they were overruled by the union executive, which authorised the talks to go ahead.

The executive reconciled the upper and lower ranks of the union through an ingenious formula that let negotiations begin, as O'Brien wanted, while apparently dissolving into thin air the 30 November deadline, as the chapels wanted. Time, or lack of it, was the thing on which top and bottom in the union could agree. If 'meaningful negotiations' were going on, the executive decided, then the company would not fire anybody. 'It is recognised', said O'Brien in a circular letter in early October, 'that the time factor will make it difficult to actually conclude all agreements by the 30th November.' By a judicious use of the passive tense – 'it is recognised' – he contrived to make it seem that the company agreed with him. But the company did not agree. It wanted signed agreements by the end of November, not 'meaningful negotiations'.

Negotiations duly began, but with the machine and clerical chapels they did not get far and never looked as if they would. Brady's chapel simply rejected the company's proposals, as bluntly when they were revised as when they were first presented. Fitzpatrick was less abrasive. He started to negotiate, painstakingly, line by line, but progress was extremely slow, and it remained so even after the company had radically reduced the number of issues on which it required agreement by the deadline.

As 30 November drew near the union sent in a senior official, John Moakes, to take charge of the union side of the clerical talks. After two meetings Moakes played the card Natsopa's executive had devised. 'Meaningful negotiations' were now taking place, he said, so the company must withdraw its threat of dismissal. But the management negotiators refused, and Moakes thereupon withdrew Fitzpatrick and the rest of the union team.

Meanwhile, another section of Natsopa, the Rirma branch, had been negotiating in an altogether different style. After an opening blast of hostility to the company's proposals, the Rirma negotiators got down to serious haggling, and by the end of November they had succeeded in making deals with the company covering ten out of the fourteen groups into which its 500 members were divided, a miscellaneous collection of staff from commissionaires to messengers, firemen to canteen cooks.

One chapel father, Tony Britton, set the pace for the others. Britton did not, at first, like the company's plans any more than the others, and he had been one of the eleven chapel fathers who signed the letter of protest to Hussey in July. But he soon turned pragmatic, seeing it as his job to avoid his members' dismissal and to get the best deal he could for them.

What the company wanted from each of the three Natsopa sections was different in detail but not so prodigiously different as to account for the relative success of the negotiations with Rirma and the complete failure of negotiations with the clerical and machine chapels. While Rirma was ready to make a deal, trading jobs against cash, the other chapels seemed more concerned with the intangibles of union power and chapel rights. The outcome of the negotiations in each section bore the unmistakable imprint of their most prominent negotiators, Brady, Fitzpatrick and Britton.

As time ran out, time itself became the issue. We cannot negotiate everything in the time you have given us, said the unions. Yes, you can, the board answered, if you really want to.

To this argument there was no end. How long is a labour negotiation? How long is a piece of string? The answers depend on what you want to do with the string or the time. Some unions, especially the Natsopa clerical chapels, chose to regard the company's proposals as infinitely complex, needing months to sort out. The company chose to see its own proposals as pretty simple, needing only a bit of determination to agree on them by the deadline.

Neither side was unanimous on the question of time or totally convinced by its own propaganda. Time was not a real problem to a union like Slade, which could have met the deadline but held back because other unions were not ready. Lack of time, on the other hand, did worry some directors like Harold Evans and Donald Cruickshank, who thought it made the company vulnerable. But, whatever their private reservations, time became the medium – like a tug-of-war rope – through which each side tested the will and the strength of the other.

Time had begun to take shape as an issue in September, when the board met the union general secretaries for the first time since April. Bill Keys and Owen O'Brien had left that meeting to tell reporters they were willing to start negotiations, but that they did not think there was enough time left to complete them.

For O'Brien time was an especially useful theme around which to harmonise the discordant ranks of his union. On 10 November he wrote to all his members at Times Newspapers reiterating that it was impracticable to reach agreement in the time left, so that it would also be irresponsible for the company to close the newspaper and dismiss the staff, or at any rate those members whose chapels were still negotiating. A week later a mass meeting endorsed his line, and at the same time O'Brien published his correspondence with Hussey and Nisbet-Smith to show that though he had been eager to negotiate for months past, the company had not.

Brady also made a gesture to win time. On the Sunday morning of 19 November he lifted an overtime ban his chapel had been operating since the summer. The ban was costing the *Sunday Times* thousands of copies a week. By lifting it, Brady reasoned, he was ceasing to exert the union's form of pressure on the company; the company should reciprocate by abandoning its own pressure – the deadline – on the unions. His gesture might also help to strengthen the arguments of Keys and O'Brien who were due to put their case for more time to Albert Booth, the Employment Secretary, on the following day, as the company's case for tough and urgent action might look convincing to Booth the day after action by Natsopa members had caused the *Sunday Times* to lose yet more thousands of copies. (The newspaper lost copies anyway through action by the NGA.)

Keys and O'Brien did their best to persuade Booth to use the Government's influence on the company. And they put their arguments again the next day, this time to Hussey, who had called them in to discuss a procedure for settling disputes. But Hussey was unmoved by Booth, Brady or the union leaders. The deadline, he said, must stay.

O'Brien kept pegging away at the theme of time. Two days before the deadline he persuaded his executive to accept Hussey's latest disputes procedure on condition that the company withdrew from the shutdown. But the company would not withdraw. The next day O'Brien made one more bid. He asked to see the Times board. It did not, he claimed, know the whole story. But again his request was refused.

Barry Fitzpatrick too found a time card to play at the next-to-last moment, the day before the deadline, when Mrs Margaret Thatcher, still Leader of the Tory Opposition but soon to be Britain's first woman Prime Minister, came to lunch at New Printing House Square. Harold Evans had invited her long before to meet some of his journalists around the table of the *Sunday Times* dining-room. As we waited, word came that clerical staff were getting ready to lobby her in the front hall. Mild panic set in. Somebody tried to contact her office, but she was already in her car and on her way. Evans waited anxiously for her on the pavement, and the company's chief security officer, a burly ex-policeman called McGorrian, stood by to escort her through the crowded hall.

But they need not have worried. The girls in the lobby were good-humoured and Mrs Thatcher, calm and cheerful, absorbed her unexpected reception with a politician's aplomb. Fitzpatrick caught up with her by the lifts and complained that that very morning, when there were barely twenty-four hours left, Nisbet-Smith had refused to see him. Would she please intervene? But Mrs Thatcher just patted Fitzpatrick on the stomach, said she was only there to meet the journalists and, still smiling, entered a lift and disappeared.

Hussey and the rest of the Times board continued to keep up their public front of implacable resolution right to the end. But the union campaign was beginning to have its effect within the board and beyond, not least in political circles, where, according to the ways of the British industrial system, any well-publicised dispute like the row at the Times is likely to develop into a hot political issue.

Aware of these ways, Hussey had been careful to keep the right people briefed. He had called on Albert Booth and Booth's deputy, Harold Walker, more than once. He had been to see Jim Prior, Booth's opposite number on the Tory benches. He was in increasingly frequent touch by telephone with Matt Wake, Booth's chief official trouble-shooter. With Mike Mander, Hussey had spoken to groups of backbench MPs from all three political parties. And he had expounded his woes to Len Murray, the TUC general secretary, offering to conduct Murray round the new technology on the third floor of the *Sunday Times* building. (Murray had turned the offer down on the grounds that in disputes in which he could play a useful mediating role ignorance of details was often the best policy.)

On the day of the deadline the dispute at the Times was aired in a three-hour emergency debate in the House of Commons. Speaker after speaker lingered on the question of time, insisting that the host of changes the company wanted were too many to be digested in only two months. Most impressively, Jim Prior took up this line. 'I think there was delay,' he said, 'and that the management is vulnerable to criticism about not getting on with the negotiations sooner. There were a number of reasons for it as we know, but management did not get on with it very quickly.'

Through his political contacts Hussey was already aware of this current, and he had the Commons debate reported back to him. In the late afternoon he assembled his boardroom colleagues, and close to seven o'clock he met waiting reporters. The company, he revealed, was now prepared to bow to what seemed to be the common opinion on time. It would continue with its plan to close down the newspaper. No *Times* would be printed that night. But he would not issue dis-

missal notices immediately. Dismissals would be postponed for two
weeks to give one last stretch of time for negotiation.

Postponing the dismissals was not something that had come to the
board in a flash of inspiration that evening. Directors had mulled it
over before. But until now they could not have afforded to admit it
in public. Even to have dropped a hint of such a possibility would
have taken all sense of urgency out of the negotiations, which would
quickly have gone as flat as a blown-out tyre. But if postponement
could not have been hinted at earlier, there were disadvantages to the
company in conceding a period of grace at the last moment. It
seemed to thrust a notable victory into the unions' hands. Their
propaganda campaign was seen to pay off. One victory would naturally encourage the unions to seek another.

And that was exactly what happened. Little of the extra fortnight
was spent in hard bargaining. Most of it was used to argue new
variations on the theme of time.

These variations developed around the idea of creating a timetable for negotiation which would extend the period of grace beyond
two weeks. The NGA was first to spring this idea, suggesting a round-
table conference, perhaps chaired by Booth, to fix the timetable;
while that was going on, the company would not dismiss anybody.
But the NGA added a condition of its own: single keystroking must
be dropped from the negotiating agenda altogether. The company
rejected this immediately, claiming to be surprised that the NGA
should propose a condition which it knew would not be acceptable
and suggesting instead an intensive weekend of negotiations 'un-
hampered by preconditions'. Kenneth Thomson made a rare public
appearance at a press conference to underline the company's attitude.
To concede on keystroking, he said, would be to give up a basic
objective. At this the NGA in turn rejected the company's proposal.

But that did not kill off the idea of a timetable. The same notion
had been busily evolving at the TUC and in Booth's office, and in discreet exchanges between the two. And a timetable (of a sort) was
rigged up in two days of talks at Booth's office, with Booth himself
acting as go-between. The timetable was supposed to start to roll at
a meeting a few days later to be chaired by Len Murray. Whether it
could have worked is doubtful. The timescale for negotiations proposed by the company was very different from the unions'. Hussey

thought negotiations should be wrapped up in little more than two weeks. Owen O'Brien thought six might do it, while Joe Wade thought it would be more like three months. But however long the timetable might be, there was one snag to be overcome first. It was now the very last day of the extra two weeks' grace the company had conceded, and dismissal notices were due to go out that night.

Both Wade and Bill Keys insisted that they could not hope to negotiate while their members were under threat of dismissal. Keys warned Hussey darkly that there were some people who did not want to see his newspapers produced again. It would be difficult enough to get them to negotiate anyway, impossible if the notices were put in the post. Wade said his members would be so resentful that there would be no way he could meet the company.

But the directors who were there refused to budge. They had already extended their deadline for dismissals by a fortnight, and the results had been extremely disappointing. Without unmistakable evidence that the company meant what it said, which only notices delivered to the staff would provide, there would be no pressure on the unions to settle. Besides, Toronto would not have allowed another postponement, and the private advice of the TUC, which was keeping in close touch with events, counselled against one too.

Nisbet-Smith took particular care to make sure that this was understood. He summoned Keys from the room in which the union leaders were meeting to ask him if they all knew exactly what the company's position was. Keys assured him that they did know – at which the directors returned to Gray's Inn Road and ordered the dismissal notices to be posted that night.

O'Brien made one last desperate bid to keep the talks going. Five days after the notices went out he gathered together his chapel officers and persuaded them that if they would agree to 'meaningful negotiations', the company would withdraw its notices. From the meeting he telephoned Hussey. 'Do you agree', he asked, 'that you said that you will withdraw notices to any chapel where meaningful discussions take place?' But Hussey said that was not possible – he had never said it. O'Brien slammed down the phone in a burst of anger.

It was now clear that the company's strategy had not worked, at any rate in its first phase. The threat of dismissal had not been enough to persuade the unions to come to terms with its proposals.

By 30 November only the *Sunday Times* journalists and the newspapers' circulation reps had reached agreements, and in the two weeks of extra time only two more groups followed, the *Times* journalists and the maintenance engineers. The most difficult unions, the NGA and Natsopa, and the most awkward departments, the clerical and the machine room, were as far from agreement as ever. (Unhappily for them, the agreements made by the Rirma chapels were not allowed to count because Natsopa did not endorse them.)

To the board the failure of the two extra weeks to produce significant progress was conclusive proof that time was not a real issue but a tactic, a means of testing the company's will. The failure toughened its determination not to make more concessions. But to the unions the two-week concession was a further reassuring sign of management weakness to add to all the others. First, the company had dropped its hard-line disputes procedure. Then it had chosen to let the staff serve out their notice, not to lock them out on the day of the deadline. Finally, it had compromised on the 30 November date. If the argument between the two sides was a contest of credibility, as it certainly seemed to have become, the management emerged from the first round looking, to union eyes, in distinctly poor shape.

With the approach of Christmas, the contestants retired to their corners. The only sign of activity was a muted traffic in anxious telephone calls between management and union officials. At a board meeting one director quipped to another: 'This could be our Waterloo.' To which the other replied: 'Yes, but who's going to be Napoleon?' On the telephone Nisbet-Smith told me that things were at their 'most silent, grimmest, darkest and most mysterious'. But, alas, he was too optimistic. The dispute was to get far grimmer and darker than any of us were yet able to imagine.

Top William Rees-Mogg, editor of the *Times*. (*photo Sally Soames*)

Sunday Times journalists give a press conference during the shutdown. The author is on the left. (*Sally Soames*)

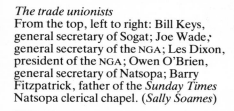

The trade unionists
From the top, left to right: Bill Keys,
general secretary of Sogat; Joe Wade,
general secretary of the NGA; Les Dixon,
president of the NGA; Owen O'Brien,
general secretary of Natsopa; Barry
Fitzpatrick, father of the *Sunday Times*
Natsopa clerical chapel. (*Sally Soames*)

The employers
From the top, left to right: Marmaduke
'Duke' Hussey, chief executive of Times
Newspapers; Kenneth Thomson, the
proprietor; Gordon Brunton, chief
executive of the Thomson Organisation;
Michael Mander, deputy chief executive
of Times Newspapers; Dugal Nisbet-
Smith, general manager of Times
Newspapers.

The night the *Sunday Times* came back.
Sir Denis Hamilton, editor-in-chief (left)
and the journalists receive their first
copies. (*Sally Soames*)

6
OUTSIDE
INTEREST

One day in November I ran into Barry Fitzpatrick in the street near the office. I asked him who was going to win the argument over the NAPS, the unions or the company, and he answered with what at the time seemed plain common sense: 'The company. They've got more money than us.'

The financial resources behind Times Newspapers dwarfed those of the print unions – indeed of the whole British trade union movement. In 1978 the trading profit of the International Thomson Organisation was £146.5 millions; the same year the total income of the twenty-nine largest British unions, each with above 100,000 members, was only £3 millions greater. Only two print unions, the NGA and Sogat, were large enough to figure among those twenty-nine. One look at the bank balances of both sides should have been enough to make the unions at the Times sue for peace.

But money was not the only index of strength. Events were to conjure up all kinds of support for the unions to lean on, though neither they nor the company foresaw how powerful those supports would be.

The first source of union strength was, ironically, the Times itself. By giving the staff notice and then extending its notice deadline for two weeks, the company ensured that the whole staff would be paid for a full month after the newspapers were shut down. Each week, from the beginning of January, the staff went off the payroll in batches as their notices expired, but the longest-serving employees were entitled to three months' notice, which would not run out until mid-March. On top of that, the company did not intend to fire those of its staff who had agreements. For more than three months, therefore, it was committed to paying about half its staff their normal earnings, and more than a quarter would stay on the payroll indefinitely.

A lockout would have made the entire work force a burden on the unions from the very first day of the shutdown. As it was, the company's milder tactics gave the unions a long breathing space in which to explore the possibilities of their second source of strength – their role as hiring agents for the print trade.

Well before 30 November the unions had begun to prepare. They had organised levies from their members in Fleet Street and beyond, and, where they could, they had kept vacancies open in other publishing houses. In their search for alternative work the unions were soon helped out by the rivals of the *Times* and the *Sunday Times*. The *Guardian*, the *Financial Times*, the *Daily* and *Sunday Telegraph* and the *Observer* all began to print extra copies and some – especially the *Observer* – extra pages and even sections; and to cope with the additional work they put more machines into operation and took on extra union labour. Almost magically, an industry that was already notoriously over-manned absorbed the staff of the *Times* and the *Sunday Times* as it came off the company's payroll. The levies the unions had raised were hardly needed, though the NGA and Slade did use their money to pay their members at the Times rate of £70 or £80 a week to stay away from work altogether. For those two unions direct financial support was not difficult. They were comparatively rich, and the numbers involved were less than 1 per cent of their memberships.

Within a very few weeks the balance of forces looked very different from how it had seemed in November. The company was no longer self-evidently stronger than the unions. Its financial power had been misleading; the unions had discovered means of resistance, and the two sides were now more evenly matched than anybody had thought possible.

As the new balance of power emerged, the nature of the argument changed subtly. Up to the November deadline the company had dictated the shape of the dispute. Either you accept our new terms, it had said to the unions, or your members will be dismissed. Now the unions began to take the initiative. You must, they said to the company, take our members back; only when they are working again will we discuss with you the new terms you want. This was the position taken up in January both by the Natsopa executive and by a new liaison committee organised by the Times chapels, with Fitzpatrick in the chair. The committee had no formal standing with the unions or the company, but it was to exercise a powerful influence on the dispute.

The company, however, was not ready to make concessions. A memo drawn up by Donald Cruickshank for the board on 11 January, headed 'Minimum requirements for resumption', showed all the company's original priorities still intact: guaranteed production, manning reductions, greater managerial powers, a programme for single keystroking and all the rest. Nor was the company ready to abandon its negotiating strategy. It still thought its best chance lay in winning the support of the union leaders for its plans before it took the plans to the chapels.

How, then, were the two sides to be reconciled? The British system of industrial relations contains several mechanisms for resolving important and intractable disputes. There is the TUC, which specialises in settling disagreements between unions and disputes which threaten a lot of union jobs; there is the Advisory, Conciliation and Arbitration Service (Acas), a countrywide corps of mediators paid for by the Government but run by a board of trade unionists and employers; and there is the Government itself, usually in the person of the Secretary for Employment, then Albert Booth.

When a dispute becomes as entrenched as that at Times Newspapers, it is a matter of tactics and timing which one of these three intervenes. The logic of events pointed to the TUC. Booth had already tried. In December he had drawn up a negotiating programme, which would have begun with a meeting chaired by Len Murray at the TUC if the unions had not rejected the programme when Hussey refused to withdraw the staff's notices. It would make sense to start again where Booth left off – at the TUC – if a new and workable negotiating programme could be devised.

The early weeks of 1979 – which became known as the 'winter of discontent' – were an awkward time for the Establishment of the Labour movement, trade unionists as well as politicians. A general election could only be a few months away, but ordinary people were being harassed by a series of strikes in services like schools and road transport as unions struggled against tight pay restrictions. However much union leaders disliked the Government's policy on pay, they liked the prospect of a Tory Government even less. Every available union hand was therefore engaged in trying to resolve the disputes in ways that would repair the damage which strikes were doing to Labour's tattered reputation without at the same time offending union members.

The heaviest burden, naturally, fell on the TUC, through whose doors marched a constant stream of union disputants. In spite of this pressure, Len Murray contrived to keep close to the Times dispute. Directors of the company and print union leaders were regular callers at his office, to the point at which they were almost tripping over other seekers of help from other beleaguered industries. On one occasion an embarrassed Murray, ensnared by groups of union leaders scattered around the TUC headquarters, asked Hussey to mind his telephone while he dealt with them, which Hussey did for almost an hour. There were, as it happened, no calls.

In industrial as in other kinds of diplomacy it is often essential to have an understanding in private before any moves are made in public. In the Times dispute the first issue that had to be cleared up was keystroking. To the company's delight, it believed it had found a path through this dilemma at a secret meeting with NGA leaders at the TUC in January.

The compromise the company proposed was to involve the union in an experiment. For a limited period three journalists and three Natsopa tele-ad girls would be allowed to work the new keyboards. Then there would be a pause while the results were reviewed. That suited the company in two ways: it would establish the principle of people other than NGA members using the keyboards; and, it was hoped, the evidence of the experiment would be so overwhelmingly in favour of the merits of working the new technology 'front-end' that there would be no going back. Hussey and Nisbet-Smith came away from their meeting with Joe Wade and Les Dixon convinced that the union leaders had agreed.

With keystroking apparently resolved, there were still all the other elements of a peace package to fit into place. Much of the work fell on Ken Graham, one of the TUC's senior officials, who knew the print trade well. Patiently, in the moments he could spare from the industrial chaos of the time, he took soundings from the union leaders and the company and began drafting an agreement. By early February, after several efforts, he had one that Hussey found acceptable and seemed worth trying out.

Graham's formula was remarkably concise. In eight short paragraphs it set out a programme of negotiations under which staff still under notice were to remain on the payroll for several more weeks, while those who had already been dismissed would receive their wages for the same number of weeks. That would keep the atmosphere sweet while hard negotiations went on over the company's demands for change, and once those negotiations were completed, everybody would get his job back. Graham had left blanks, particularly in connection with the timescale, but on the whole it seemed an adept stab at summarising the common ground of opinion within the unions and the company.

The formula, however, contained a trap. The word Graham had used for giving staff their jobs back was 're-engagement'; but the chapels were by now calling for 'reinstatement'. There was an important difference between the two. 'Reinstatement' meant giving staff their jobs back in full, as though they had never been fired or given notice, which in turn meant that if the negotiations went sour, staff members would have to be given their notices all over again. The company could find itself paying wages for three more months of idleness. Hussey was fully alive to the significance of 'reinstatement', which was why he had accepted the more tentative 're-engagement'. Graham had become sensitive to the nuances of the dispute and he was still casting about for ways around the problem when the worst happened. His formula leaked.

Graham's single-page document had been given only a limited circulation around the unions and the company; the precise source of the leak remains mysterious. I heard about it on the morning of 7 February, when a colleague, John Fryer, rang to say that Jacob – 'Jake' – Ecclestone, the father of the *Times* journalists' chapel, had found a copy of an 'initiative' of Len Murray's lying around in a corridor of the *Times* office. When I read it, it seemed at least plausibly authentic. But when reporters asked Murray and Hussey to confirm that it was genuine, they were turned away with evasive answers. I called a TUC official who I knew had had a hand in the drafting and he was equally evasive, but then he gave the game away by asking what I thought of it. I said the company might find it hard to take because it would involve paying their full earnings to staff for a period of three months or more during which the newspapers had earned no revenue. But he thought it would cause more difficulties with the unions. 'There are some people on the union side', he said, 'who not only want the management to lie down so that they can roll over them, but who want the company to commit suicide too.'

Whether or not he was right about the motives of individuals, he was certainly right to be wary of union reaction. The day after the leak the chapel liaison committee met and rejected the TUC's proposal on the grounds that it did not include reinstatement. Ecclestone proposed the motion, and Reg Brady seconded it. Murray was furious. He had planned to meet the union leaders and, as the leading trade unionist in the country, to put the full weight of his authority behind the peace formula. But once the chapel fathers had voted against it, the TUC's initiative ran out of momentum. The general secretaries met at the TUC and agreed to recommend the formula to their executives – all except Joe Wade, who said he would put it to his executive but would not recommend it. The following week the NGA duly turned it down.

With that the TUC's intervention was dead. The leak had effectively sabotaged its initiative by letting the liaison committee have the first word before Murray could recommend his scheme to the union leaders. The TUC did not fade from the scene altogether, but the fact that it had been publicly rebuffed made further intervention from that quarter far more difficult.

Over the first weekend in March the Times board was in almost permanent session, meeting daily from Friday to Sunday. There were only a few days left before the last notices ran out on the remaining thousand or so of the company's longest-serving employees. Was this an opportunity for the company to seize? It might be; but what was the company actually to do? The most hotly debated idea was for Denis Hamilton to meet the liaison committee of chapel fathers. The fathers would, after all, have to be brought into the negotiations at some point. But the new committee was regarded with suspicion by the union leaders Some saw it as potentially yet another source of power to obstruct their own; others regarded it as a group of political trouble-makers. And the company did not want to offend the union leaders because it still saw them as the most likely route to agreement.

Besides, the advice coming through from Albert Booth's Department and from the TUC was to do nothing. Moves were being prepared by both, and any action by the company could upset them. The TUC wanted to use the last dismissals as an excuse for summoning the union leaders for a new round of peace-making. But, to the TUC's annoyance, Booth intervened ahead of that critical date. The companys too, was sceptical about Booth, but it would not have been good politics for it to be seen to turn down the help of a Labour Minister.

Booth, in his early fifties, looked something like the popular idea of an English policeman or a sergeant-major: tall, rubicund, straight-backed, hair neatly parted and cut short around the neck and ears. A draughtsman sponsored in Parliament by the white-collar section of the engineering union, his political background was that of the Tribune group, the orthodox Labour left. But his stolid appearance and plain, sometimes hesitant, way of speaking did not tell his whole story. His large hands were said to be nimble on a stringed instrument, and his mind was certainly agile when it came to reading the quirks of an industrial dispute.

There had been a time when the job which Booth held was one of the most prominent in Government. Reporters and television cameras frequently waited into the night at the Employment Secretary's office in St James's Square, while he wrestled with employers and unions to bring peace to one great industry or another. But by the 1970s the unions had become suspicious of Government conciliation, fearing that the Employment Secretary would use his good offices only to press on them the Government's latest attempt to keep down pay increases. Acas had been set up to assume the role of an independent national mediator. It had taken over the Employment Department's staff, and the Secretary of State was now rarely seen to intervene. Booth had become publicly embroiled in only one dispute, a strike of helicopter pilots who serviced the North Sea oil rigs and whose dispute threatened the all-important flow of oil to Britain. With the TUC's failure and his own political reputation in mind,

Booth approached intervention in the Times dispute with particular care.

Like Graham at the TUC, Booth and his senior adviser, Matt Wake, had kept in regular touch with the company and the unions, and from the buzz of signals on which they eavesdropped it appeared by the end of February that both sides were ready to have another try at making peace. The NGA, though, was still cagey, and Booth had no wish to fall flat at the first hurdle by calling the two sides together only to find that the NGA would not come. He would have to sound its leaders out first. Dick Seaman, his information director, happened to know one of the managers at the Cavendish Hotel, once the domain of the eccentric hotel keeper Rosa Lewis but now rebuilt as a conventional luxury block and conveniently close to Booth's office, just around the corner in Jermyn Street. Seaman reserved a discreet private room for Monday, 5 March, and Joe Wade and Les Dixon agreed to come to lunch.

Two points emerged at the lunch, one encouraging to Booth, the other less so. The first was that the NGA would come to a meeting if Booth issued the invitation. Wade and Dixon were under instructions not to talk to the company until it offered NGA members reinstatement; but the union executive had not forbidden them to talk to Booth. The second point was the price which the NGA expected the company to pay. Not only did it want all its members to have their jobs back at the Times, but it wanted them to have all the money they had missed as a result of being fired as well.

Booth chose to be encouraged. He and Wake returned to St James's Square, and Wake immediately began to rough out a new peace formula – which was not, in fact, all that fresh; it was a reworking of the elements of a timetable which had already been tried out in one design by the TUC and in an earlier version by Booth himself. When Booth was satisfied with Wake's draft, it was outlined to Hussey over the telephone. Next day, Tuesday, Hussey reported what he had heard to the board. Booth, he said, had asked him to go to his office and talk about it that afternoon. The board agreed that he should go. Hussey took Mike Mander, Dugal Nisbet-Smith and Donald Cruickshank with him, and the four men listened while Booth went through his ideas, not showing them Wake's draft but sketching out his proposals with a certain deliberate imprecision. Hussey was equally imprecise in his response, but he agreed to return the next day if the union leaders came too. That was all Booth wanted for the moment; he told his officials to contact the unions and to confirm the meeting which the union leaders had already been warned to expect.

Next afternoon Booth finished off some business in his large, second-floor office looking out over the square before he stepped into the conference room next door, where the union leaders were waiting for him. Booth again sketched out his proposals, and although Wade and Dixon did not seem as flexible as they had been at lunch two days before, he thought it worth summoning Hussey from Gray's Inn Road, where he was waiting for a call. At about seven o'clock Hussey and the same three directors he had brought the day before arrived at Booth's office. Booth told them briefly how he intended to run the negotiation, and then moved into the conference room to join the trade unionists: five general secretaries, each with a colleague, apart from Ken Ashton of the NUJ, who had come alone. After Hussey had walked around the table shaking the trade unionists by the hand, Booth opened the meeting.

Wake's formula set out a timetable for negotiations, with a target date at the end for restarting the newspapers. This time around the staff who had lost their jobs would be taken back on contracts that would keep them on the payroll until the target date, while those who had not yet gone would have their notices extended to the same date. That was the sweetener to get negotiations going, and if the negotiations were successful, then of course all the staff would be kept permanently on the payroll. In addition, staff who came back to the company would get some of the earnings they had lost immediately and the rest when the newspapers were restarted.

Several lessons had been learned from the TUC's failure. Wake's timetable was tighter and more exact. He had been careful to specify that it was reinstatement, and not just re-engagement, that was on offer. And Booth kept Wake's draft strictly to himself. For it must surely have been through one of the men present in the conference room that the TUC's initiative had been leaked and had consequently been aborted, and Booth was determined not to give that man a second chance. He was to speak from the draft, but half a dozen re-drafts were written, and several hours passed before Booth felt its safe to let anyone but himself and his officials have a copy in their hands.

It did not take very long for the snag in Wake's formula to surface. How much of their lost wages should dismissed staff be paid as soon as they returned to work, and how much should be kept back until the papers were restarted? The company wanted to keep back as much as possible so as to keep up the pressure on the unions to settle. Hussey therefore offered to pay 25 per cent down and the rest later. Joe Wade's response was angry. 'If that's all you can offer, it's no good,' he said. 'That's all there is,' replied Hussey. 'That's it,' said Wade, and he began to gather together his papers and push his chair away from the table. For perhaps twenty seconds there was silence, broken only by the sound of Nisbet-Smith puffing at his pipe. It looked like a sharp, sad end to Booth's intervention. But then Booth himself came to the rescue. He began to talk about something else. Wade looked nonplussed, but he pulled his chair back up to the table and joined in the discussion. After a quarter of an hour Booth dissolved the meeting. His adroit switch of topic had saved the day, and the incident had also revealed which was the most delicate issue in the peace plan.

If it had done nothing else, that session had shown just how difficult the NGA was likely to be. Booth was pessimistic and even thought of calling off his initiative. But Hussey knew the print unions' form. Once he had negotiated a Fleet Street dispute with Vic Feather, Len Murray's predecessor at the TUC, and had come to a swift agreement. Hussey was all for reporting straight back to the union leaders who were waiting for them, but Feather insisted that they share a bottle of whisky first. It would not do to be hasty, according to Feather; print unions expected their problems to take time to solve. Time was what they expected that night too, Hussey suggested.

Booth now agreed a new tactic. The union leaders would stay where they were in the conference room, and the Times directors would withdraw along the corridor to another office, room 202. There the two sides would stay, firmly apart, and Booth and his officials would commute between them. It would drag the negotiations out, but that was what the union leaders expected; and it would avoid the dangers of face-to-face confrontation which the row between Hussey and Wade had revealed all too clearly.

From what he knew of Booth's plans, Bill Keys was alert to the possibility that the way in which the money was paid to the staff for coming back to work might be the most difficult issue, and before the negotiations opened he had whispered to Wake that a fifty-fifty deal would be the best way out: half the money down and the rest later. With the two sides apart, Wake tried it out on Hussey, who agreed. Wake then sent in a message to Keys that he was wanted on the telephone. When Keys came out to take the call, he found there was none. Instead he found Wake, who asked him to put the fifty-fifty deal to the other union leaders as though it came from Booth. Keys said he would. He returned to the conference room and put it to his colleagues. They quickly endorsed the compromise and sent a message along the corridor to room 202: fifty-fifty, take it or leave it. Hussey replied that he would take it.

With this neatly contrived deal the back of the negotiation was broken. There were still plenty of details to settle, and it took time to settle them. Talks dragged into the night as Booth and Wake jogged between the directors and the union leaders, and as one draft followed another. What, for instance, should be the target date for publication? Early drafts spoke vaguely of a five-week period, and it was not until the last draft but one that a firm date for starting up the *Times* again, 17 April, was written in. Drink was denied the two sides, Booth having no wish to allow anybody's judgement to become clouded, until at 10 o'clock it was reckoned safe. Beer, gin and whisky were wheeled in, the same for each team. Mike Mander dug into his pocket and gave £35 to his driver with orders to find food. Adding £10 of his own, the driver returned with fish, chips and salami, which the directors shared with the union leaders. Booth and his officials dined less well, off hamburgers from McDonald's. By the early hours of the morning the rooms were awash with scraps of paper, overflowing ashtrays, empty beer bottles – the usual detritus of a long negotiation. Dick Seaman found Bill Miles, of Sogat, wandering the corridor in search of a dictionary to check the spelling of a word he thought might make an anagram in a *Financial Times* crossword. The word was 'enema'. It did not fit.

At long last, after some eight versions of Wake's original draft had been typed – nobody could remember afterwards exactly how many versions there had been – Booth summoned the Times directors to join him and the union leaders in the conference room. And there, just before 3.30 a.m., Hussey and each of the general secretaries put their signatures to the very last draft. The union leaders congratulated Booth, and Hussey promised him the first copy of the *Times* to roll off the presses on 17 April. It was, said Hussey, an historic night in the long history of the *Times*.

In the early hours of the morning euphoria was understandable. Booth had achieved something that had evaded him in December and the TUC in February. There was now an agreed timetable for negotiations, leading up to a date for publication. Talks about talks were over; talks proper could began. But on the real issues of technology, jobs, pay and all the rest of the company's demands there was no evidence that the two sides were any closer than they had been in November. Euphoria might still prove premature.

The issue of single keystroking, for instance, was as difficult as ever. If anything, each side had hardened its line. Since November the NGA's insistence that nobody but its own members should operate the new keyboards had been powerfully reinforced by the decisions of other newspapers. In January the *Glasgow Herald* had abruptly dropped its plans to let journalists work keyboards. The same month the *Observer* announced that it was installing electronic systems designed to leave keyboards under NGA control. And soon afterwards the *Express* made a proposal to the NGA so similar to the *Observer*'s that it aroused profound suspicion at Times Newspapers. Perhaps it was an accident of timing that led a row of newspapers to fall into line with NGA attitudes in the early months of 1979, but the cumulative effect was to make Times Newspapers look the odd man out in the print trade.

But the company was more determined than ever to achieve its aims. In November it had been ready to remove single keystroking from its deadline package, reckoning that it was not worth closing the newspapers on that issue alone. Now, four months and several million pounds later, it had changed its mind. The NGA must agree to a programme that would lead to the granting of some access to the keyboards to people who were not its members, or there would be no publication on 17 April and no jobs for NGA members at the Times.

There was a brief outburst of optimism among directors that the NGA was bending towards a compromise early in April. Dugal Nisbet-Smith had written to Les Dixon suggesting that journalists and tele-ad girls be phased in to the keyboards. The tele-ad girls would start using them one year after the NGA and the journalists two years. Even then the process would be gradual. Journalists would only edit copy on the keyboards to start with; they would not write stories. Nisbet-Smith's letter spoke reassuringly about the company's 'abandoning' its original plans, and it seemed to do the trick. Dixon rang Nisbet-Smith and Hussey to say that the letter was very helpful. A meeting was arranged for 4 April, which the company expected would be little more than a formality followed by a celebration.

The meeting began cheerfully, with Dixon repeating that Nisbet-Smith's letter had been very helpful. But then Dixon went on to repudiate almost every practical point in it. There could be no access for anybody but NGA members after one year or two, even for limited editing by journalists. All Dixon would agree to was that there could be a review after three years, instead of the five years he had offered to other newspapers, and even then he would not commit himself to an outcome that would let journalists use the keyboards. Nisbet-Smith was outraged at what he felt was a complete reversal by Dixon, and he told him so. But it was no use. Dixon meant what he said; the NGA would not budge.

The union's underlying attitudes were spelled out in a telephone conversation the following day between one of its senior officials and a director, who made notes of what passed.

> I know what you want [the union official said]. We have to sell it very privately, and very sincerely we have to put a stop on it for a period of time. You are getting away with 45 per cent of the jobs – we can't give our birthright away at the same time. We must have a period with no inputting. Once that is over, you will get it, I can promise you, you will get it.

What he meant was that moving from hot metal to 'cold type' would cost the NGA nearly half its jobs at the Times, the union could not be expected to give up its control of the keyboards – its 'birthright' – as well; there would have to be an interval, but once it was over, the company could have its journalists keyboard to their heart's content. Like St Augustine, the NGA was willing to change its ways, but not just yet.

The company, however, wanted some real guarantees that the NGA

would change. There was not now much time left before the publication date, and the argument between Nisbet-Smith and Dixon
shifted to the Westminster offices of Acas, to which the Booth plan
had delegated the task of mediating any last-minute hitches. The
company whittled away its demands, trying one ingenious formula
after another in a desperate effort to find a way to reconcile its determination to ensure that there would be some access to the new keyboards for staff who were not NGA members with the NGA's insistence
that there should be no such access at all.

One suggestion was that tele-ad girls should take down advertisements on terminals. The advertisements would then be transferred
to terminals operated by NGA men, where they would appear on one
half of a split screen. NGA operators would re-keyboard the words on
the other half of the screen, and it would be their keystrokes that
would actually set the words in type. Another suggestion was that
journalists could use the terminals to produce paper printouts, not
photographic type, leaving NGA operators to keyboard the journalists'
work into type from the printouts. But Dixon rejected each compromise, for they all breached the NGA's principle of retaining exclusive control of the keyboards. After three days of listening to the
arguments, one Acas official was heard to murmur: 'The NGA has got
religion.'

Once again other negotiations languished under the shadow of the
wrangle over new technology. Slade and Sogat could almost certainly
have made deals with the company, but they held back, as before.
With Natsopa too there was little progress. From its machine chapels
there came the familiar rejection of the company's proposals, while
from the clerical chapels there was the same leaden-footed negotiation which amounted to the same thing. On 2 April Hussey wrote
to James Prior: 'Just to keep you up to date, I went to see Albert
Booth on Friday and told him that I thought unless there was a
change in the attitude of Fitzpatrick and Brady there was no chance
of these papers appearing on April 17th, nor for a very long time
after that.'

At Acas Hussey and Nisbet-Smith had one last try at making a
deal with Dixon. They suggested they take the new technology to an
arbitrator and bind themselves to accept his findings. Dixon was not
keen, but he was persuaded to put it to his union's executive. On 19

April the executive turned it down. That decision, two days after the target date for publication had passed, was confirmation that Booth's initiative had failed conclusively.

In its five-week life the Booth programme brought only one new group of Times staff to full agreement with the company, the electricians. Those weeks were almost an action replay of the first round of negotiations in the autumn. In April, as in November, the company failed to establish its credibility with the unions, persuading them neither of the benefits of its innovations nor of the penalties for rejecting them. Technology exercised psychological dominion over every other issue; as a result, only a trickle of staff were induced to make settlements. After Booth, as after the November deadline, those groups that had come to terms with the company were the ones with whom the company had the least quarrel; the knottiest problems were still left to be unravelled. The unions, far from being cowed by the five-month shutdown, were more confident than ever, a fact which made even those differences between the two sides that had seemed minor in November looked monstrously large in April.

To break out of the impasse, it seemed to some in the company, would take something altogether new and different. Conventional methods had been exhausted; it was time to try shock tactics. The company now embarked on an adventure that was to remove the struggle to strange territory, to an environment wholly unlike that of Gray's Inn Road, into an atmosphere of deep hostility and even of terror.

7
TERROR
IN
FRANKFURT

Frankfurt airport is a huge, joyless place, whose impersonal comforts include a sex cinema and pedestrian access, across a 100-foot bridge of iron girders stretched above airport roadways, to a Sheraton hotel. On arrival, a traveller picks up his luggage and, if he is making for the Sheraton, rises two floors by escalator to the bridge. Just in from London in the late evening of Thursday, 26 April, Karin Dahmen, a member of the *Times*'s marketing staff, was riding up the first escalator when she was struck on the head by one of two men who were standing together just ahead of her on the second escalator.

The configuration of the escalators allowed time for only one blow before the men were carried away out of range. Karin Dahmen put her hand to her head and felt a trickle of blood. The incident was upsetting, but it did not seem serious. She crossed the bridge, signed into the hotel and went to her room. Then the wound opened and began to bleed badly. Not wanting to disturb Mike Mander, the most senior Times executive at the hotel, she called Clive Lovesy, the *Times*'s circulation manager, who came to her room. He stayed with her for three-quarters of an hour, but when the bleeding failed to stop, he made an excuse and went in search of Mander, whom he found in the hotel coffee shop eating a sandwich with a BBC television reporter, Prakash Mirchandani. Lovesy took Mander aside and told him what had happened. Mander asked him to call a doctor and rushed to Karin Dahmen's room.

Mander found her soaked in blood all down her right side. The bathroom was also covered with blood. The two doctors who came said that she had two wounds, one on her head behind her right ear and the other on the ear itself, the latter a cut so severe that her earlobe was almost detached. She must go to hospital, they said, to have her ear stitched and to check that she had no internal head injuries.

Lovesy took her to hospital and brought her back in the early hours of the morning. She was shaken but all right, and later she agreed to stay on with the Times team in Frankfurt. When he had seen her to her room, Lovesy called in on Mander. The two men agreed that the attack, though gruesome, must have been a piece of mindless violence. There was no motive, no robbery or sexual assault. But by the following Sunday events had cast doubt on this comforting assumption. Mander aired his new doubts in a statement: 'One must now wonder whether this was in fact the isolated mugging we had thought at the time.'

The Times team had come to Frankfurt to publish an international edition. In London the unions had denounced it as a 'scab' paper, an attempt to undermine their stand against the company, and the NGA had alerted its opposite number in Germany, IG Druck and Papier, which had rallied its members to block publication. There had been intimidating scenes at the printing works, including what appeared to be an attempt to blow up the plant.

By coming to Frankfurt, Times Newspapers had unwittingly exposed members of its staff to the violent underside of European politics. Karin Dahmen was herself German, brought over to help the Times team with the language. Could it be that she had been identified and attacked as a warning? The two men have never been caught, and it seems unlikely that they could have known who she was. But in the nervous, jittery mood of that weekend, Mander's doubts seemed only too plausible.

The Thomson Organisation had from the start insisted that the Times must have some alternatives to fall back on if the 'big bang' solution to its problems did not work. Actually printing a newspaper in defiance of unions was a well-known way of breaking out of deadlock in the industry all over the world. There was no chance of doing that in Gray's Inn Road and little better chance anywhere else in Britain, since the unions' writ ran throughout the country. But it might be done abroad, and if it were a success, it might just jolt the unions into a compromise.

Even if it did not achieve that, publication abroad had several merits. It would give underemployed journalists and commercial staff something useful to do. It would reassert the existence of the

Times, especially among foreign advertisers, whose business ac-
counted for more than a third of advertising sales, and among overseas readers, who had regularly bought 35,000 copies a day. And it
would allow the editor, Rees-Mogg, to pronounce on the British
general election, which was only a few weeks off. While the target
date of 17 April for restarting the *Times* under Booth's plan still
looked likely, the option of an international edition stayed in the
background; but as meeting the date appeared increasingly improb-
able, the option became correspondingly more attractive.

Mander embarked on a series of overnight excursions around
Europe which were kept strictly secret, so secret that other board
members did not know about them. 'Tomorrow I shall be in the
office,' he would say mysteriously, 'but tomorrow night I shall be in
Reykjavik.' In fact, he never went to Iceland, but he did go to
Geneva, Zurich, Hamburg and Paris, and he was in touch with contacts in several other countries.

His search for a printer was hampered by the stringent specifi-
cations he was trying to meet. The printer had to be able to produce
80,000 copies of a sixteen-page newspaper, in English, at a price that
would earn a profit for the company; he would have to be located
near a major airport from which the newspaper could be quickly
distributed around Europe and North America; and he must operate
a union shop (Mander had no wish to be accused of running for the
cover of a non-union house).

There were problems everywhere. Switzerland required lengthy
formalities before it would issue work permits to Times staff. Holland
had no suitable printing plant available. But in Hamburg, on the
night of 6 April, Mander picked up a strong lead. One of his contacts, a senior executive of the Springer group, suggested he try the
Frankfurt subsidiary of the Instanbul daily, *Tercuman*. The Frankfurt works of the Tercuman company used up only three hours out of
every twenty-four printing 65,000 copies of the Turkish newspaper
for sale among the million or more exiled Turks in Europe, so it
must have capacity to spare. Through his Springer contact, Mander
made an appointment with Tercuman. Then he flew back to London,
went on to Nice for a weekend conference of *Sunday Times* advertising executives and flew back into Frankfurt on Monday evening.

The Tercuman plant at once struck Mander as promising. Its site, in a pleasant estate, part residential and part industrial, carved from a forest at Zeppelinheim, was only ten minutes from Frankfurt airport. The European edition of the newspaper was produced from negatives flown in daily from Instanbul, and since it was already a day old by the time it was printed in Frankfurt, speed of distribution was as essential for Tercuman as it would be for an international *Times*. Tercuman could print Mander's newspaper, but it had no typesetting capacity. Before returning to London, therefore, Mander outlined a tentative deal: Tercuman could have the contract on condition it found somebody who could set the newspaper in type.

What Mander did not know was that Tercuman's Frankfurt operation had already been threatened with violence. In the spectrum of Turkish politics the newspaper stands on the right, and two years earlier the man who ran the Frankfurt plant, Serhat Ilicak, had received threatening letters from an extreme left-wing Turkish group. Ilicak, a member of the family who owned the newspaper, had come to Frankfurt to study in 1970, had married there and had stayed on in the city. When he showed the threatening letters to the police, he was advised to take a number of precautions. Ilicak had had his Jaguar specially reinforced; he often drove in another car (his wife's or an employee's); he varied his routes as much as possible; and whenever he could, he tried to make sure that he did not travel alone.

Unaware of all this, Mander returned to Frankfurt a week later, bringing with him Paul Crowe, the *Times*'s production director. Ilicak had looked at three possible typesetters and was ready to recommend one, Otto Gutfreund and Son, of Darmstadt. Mander and Crowe made the half-hour journey down the autobahn to Gutfreund's plant in a grimy industrial suburb to see for themselves. By comparison with the scale of things in Gray's Inn Road, Gutfreund's seemed meagre indeed. The small three-floor building was half-empty. Three old Linotypes, unused for years, stood like museum pieces in what had once been a hot-metal composing room. Most of the firm's typesetting work was done by a team of eight women working at home on perforators, which punched tape that was brought back to Gutfreund's and processed through electronic terminals; these produced a different tape that was fed into the photosetters. To non-technicians used only to Fleet Street production methods it was to be a source of constant wonder that such a small

outfit with so little equipment and so few people could produce a
newspaper at all. But Mander and Crowe satisfied themselves that it
could do the job, even though Gutfreund's had never actually produced a newspaper – most of its work being in books and magazines
– and its staff did not speak English.

As secrecy still seemed imperative, Mander held out to Otto
Gutfreund himself the prospect of a regular contract without telling
him which newspaper it was he would be printing. Because they
negotiated through an interpreter, Mander assumed he did not know
any English. But Gutfreund had spent several years working as a
compositor in Canada in the early 1950s, long enough to avoid his
military service and to save money to start his own business at home
– and to pick up the language. Four days later, when Mander returned to confirm the contract, Gutfreund turned to him, smiling, and
asked: 'How is the London *Times*?' Eavesdropping through the
language barrier, Gutfreund must have thought, could only help his
bargaining position.

Between them, Ilicak and Gutfreund seemed able to meet
Mander's requirements. They could set and print 80,000 copies of a
sixteen-page newspaper for some £12,000, which should turn a
modest profit. Even the question of union membership looked
reasonably good. All Ilicak's printers, Mander had been assured,
were members of one or another Turkish union, and some also belonged to the German print union. Some, though not all, of Gutfreund's staff of thirty-two were union members; exactly how many
was not clear. But it was unlikely that Fleet Street's idea of a closed
shop could be found anywhere in Europe, where written national
constitutions generally guarantee both the right to belong to a union
and the right to opt out. Besides, in Germany the employers had rejected a claim for a closed shop, put forward by IG Druck and Papier
the year before in spite of its doubtful legality, after a bitterly fought
dispute.

As the prospects for the Booth initiative grew dimmer in the early
days of April, talk of alternatives flourished – and so did rumours.
The company might abandon Gray's Inn Road and its whole labour
force for a new site and a new production staff. Or it might try to
print abroad. Or it might look for a new owner. Harold Evans canvassed the idea of getting out something about the general election

at least, even if only through the *Sunday Times Reporter*, an irregular sheet covering the dispute which the journalists' chapel had started up. William Rees-Mogg wrote a paper to the board suggesting the unions be bypassed and employment contracts offered to individuals instead. On 19 April I made a puzzled note: 'Things are happening but by no means does any sort of clear picture yet emerge.'

In fact, on that same day the decision to go ahead with the Frankfurt issue had been made by the *Times* executive board. The exact status of that decision was to become a subject of controversy among directors, and it was to change the way in which the whole dispute was handled by the management. Some directors were later to claim that the only thing to have been authorised by Gordon Brunton was a feasibility study on European publication to be discussed at a meeting on 25 April; others insisted that everybody who should have been involved in the decision was involved. It is certainly true that on 23 April Hussey, responding to anxious inquiries from the Organisation's headquarters in Stratford Place, summoned a group of directors to discuss whether the Frankfurt project should be abandoned. It is also true that two days later, at a lunch in the *Times* dining-room, Brunton pointedly asked the executive board to record a formal decision to go ahead. It did, but only committed itself to one issue instead of the weekly editions over three months which Mander had already suggested in letters to Ilicak and Gutfreund.

The confusion probably sprang from the secrecy with which the Frankfurt issue was planned. At any rate, things had gone too far for the company to be able easily to back out. On 20 April, the day after the decision had been taken, Rees-Mogg informed Jake Ecclestone that an international edition was to be produced, though he stopped short of revealing where. Journalists would not have to work on it if they had a conscientious objection, Rees-Mogg said, but he was confident that enough would be willing to make production of the paper possible. (In the event, one journalist at least was to square his conscience by writing an article but withholding his by-line so that nobody would know.)

By lunchtime that day the project was common knowledge. It added to the bitter mood of a meeting of the chapels' liaison committee in the Furniture Trades Hall in Jockey Fields, a few hundred yards from the newspaper offices. The mood was already soured by the failure of the Booth initiative, which meant that staff who had been brought back on the payroll would now have to leave it again. NGA fathers struck a particularly hard line. They announced that they intended to put a picket on each of seven entrances to the two buildings in Gray's Inn Road from the following Monday, the first physical demonstration of resistance by any union since the shutdown, which was now nearly five months old.

The NGA's decision to mount pickets added one more to the pile of problems that now faced the journalists of both newspapers. Should we work on foreign editions which other unions opposed? Should we go through the picket lines which the NGA expected us to observe? We were journalists, and we wanted to be back in print; but we were, most of us, trade unionists, and we wanted to do the right thing by other unions. We were also employees of Times Newspapers, which would have a perfect right not to continue paying us if we neither worked nor crossed picket lines – and we wanted to be paid.

As it happened, the journalists' union, the NUJ, was to hold its annual conference the following week, the same week in which the international *Times* was to be prepared for printing. Meeting in Ayr in Scotland on Monday, 23 April, the union executive decided to instruct Times journalists not to work on any issue which other unions opposed. Next day the chapels of both newspapers met to make their own decisions. For *Sunday Times* journalists the conflicting problems were fairly simple to resolve. Over the weekend Harold Evans had decided not to attempt a special election edition of his newspaper, whether through the *Sunday Times Reporter* or in any other way. We could therefore go through picket lines in good conscience, knowing that we would not be doing any work on a newspaper which other unions would see as a 'scab' journal. We could go on drawing our pay – and our expenses. For us the path of virtue had been made easy.

For journalists on the *Times* the problem was altogether more agonising. They faced a real conflict of loyalties because they had a genuine prospect of publication to contend with. Some had already written articles for the international paper. Others had travelled secretly to Frankfurt to help get the paper out. Their chapel meeting was long and tortuous. So many versions of the company's motives were cited that a delegation was dispatched to see Rees-Mogg and find out the truth. It returned with a report that the main aim was to show that the *Times* was still alive. In the end, by a handful of votes, the chapel decided not to oppose publication.

In their efforts to avoid falling out with either side in the dispute, the *Times* journalists began to open up a dialogue with the NGA, which was to have important consequences and to which I shall return. But for the moment the obvious significance of the chapel vote was more important. It eliminated the last outstanding obstacle within the company to publication of the *Times* abroad.

Other unions, however, were powerfully opposed to it, especially the NGA. Les Dixon called the plan 'foolish' and a 'non-starter', and he undertook to arouse international action to stop it through the Swiss-based International Graphical Federation (IGF), a grouping of print unions in more than thirty countries to which the NGA belonged. The NGA cabled the IGF, which in turn passed on the NGA's request for solidarity against the Times to unions all over Europe, including IG Druck and Papier.

Not surprisingly, union opposition increased the company's secretiveness. As long as the unions did not know where the printer was, they could hardly stop publication. Elaborate security precautions were mounted. Only staff who needed to know were told that the printer was in Frankfurt. The staff team that began to build up in Frankfurt over the weekend made a point of never travelling directly between Darmstadt and Zeppelinheim, always going from typesetter to printer by way of their hotel or the airport. In London Mander carefully scattered the rear seat of his car with tourist guides to Zurich and Amsterdam, hoping that an inquisitive trade unionist – perhaps one of the new NGA pickets – might peer in through the window and be overcome by a false scent.

Secrecy, among those unused to practising it, can turn into something like farce. Mander had established a headquarters in a suite at the Sheraton, to which he commuted daily, working in his London office through the day and returning to Frankfurt each night. From Wednesday, 25 April he intended to stay put in Frankfurt until he had seen the international *Times* into print at the weekend; and, having escaped detection so far, he was determined to remain unnoticed on his final flight. He drove to Heathrow airport in a suede coat, one that had been a *Sunday Times* 'special offer', a corduroy sailing cap and a pair of dark glasses. At the security barrier he was asked to remove his cap. It might, after all, have concealed a bomb. Feeling a little foolish, he took off both cap and glasses once he reached the executive lounge. Immediately he recognised a director from the Mirror Group, Joe May. Thinking he had not been spotted, Mander went to the telephone – only to feel a friendly hand descend on his shoulder. It belonged to another newspaper executive, Tom Garrod of the *Daily Mail*.

Mander chatted to Garrod for a few minutes and then, when flights to Amsterdam and Geneva were announced, made his excuses and left, restoring his cap and glasses and hanging about Gate 11 until the flight he really wanted, the one to Frankfurt, was called. Much to his dismay, he spotted Garrod and May on board the same plane. Mander sent Garrod a note apologising for his unsociability, saying that he had a connection to make at Frankfurt – which was true, though the connection was with a car – and offering to call him in the morning. Garrod's reply was even more dismaying; he too was staying at the Sheraton. May and Garrod were bound for a technical conference near the airport. And when Mander got to his hotel and checked with the switchboard, he was still more dismayed to learn that Garrod was installed in room 866, directly across the passage from his own suite. But he need not have worried. Garrod had not spotted him. When a *Daily Mail* reporter, John Edwards, arrived in the Sheraton later in the week, it was not Garrod who had tipped him off.

By then the Frankfurt location was well-known. The day after the *Times* announced it was going abroad, the *Guardian* carried a story naming Frankfurt as the likely place, deducing its tip from rumours about the movements of editorial executives. Journalists and union officials followed up the tip, using the old-fashioned reporter's technique of phoning around until they had found their man. When asked, Gutfreund and Ilicak owned up, and by Thursday, 26 April their involvement in the scheme was public knowledge.

As soon as Gutfreund and Tercuman had been identified, the German union asked both companies for access to their staffs. The two companies agreed. On Thursday, accompanied by John Willats, an NGA official who had flown out to help put his union's case, IG Druck officers spoke first to Gutfreund's staff and then to Tercu-

man's. By some accounts, they laid it on pretty thick. They said that
the wives and families of Times employees in London were starving
because of the shutdown. They warned Gutfreund that the international edition he had been contracted to set was just a manoeuvre
to weaken the unions' position in London, and that as soon as Times
Newspapers had achieved that aim, it would drop him completely.
Whatever the union officials did say, it evidently had little impact on
the employees of either company, who worked as they were instructed throughout the week.

That evening George Vine, the Reuters correspondent, put a story
on the wire saying, 'West German trade union officials failed tonight
to persuade printers to "black" the paper.' A *New York Times* reporter read the story back to Mander at the Sheraton next morning,
and it seemed to Mander to confirm all the advice he had received
from his colleagues in the German printing trade. IG Druck would
make a lot of noise, but it would not succeed in stopping his publication. A few pickets had turned out at Gutfreund's on Thursday,
and a rather larger number appeared at Tercuman on Friday, but
they were peaceful enough, and they did not worry Mander. There
seemed every reason to be confident now that the international *Times*
could be printed as planned.

By Friday, though, the news that the *Times* intended to print in
Germany had received worldwide publicity, and reporters and television crews were gathering to cover the event. It was possible that
the publicity they gave it would turn an otherwise humdrum piece of
newspaper production into a drama. The presence of the media
might raise the temperature and create precisely the sort of clash the
company wanted to avoid. Mander therefore readjusted his plans.
The bulk of the 80,000 copies of the international *Times* would be
printed between 9 p.m. and midnight on Saturday. But the media
would not be told that. Instead, they would be invited to watch and
film a second press run of 25,000 copies at 11 a.m. on Sunday, which
they would be led to believe was the first and only run. That way
British television crews would have some useful footage that would
satisfy them – and would, incidentally, publicise the *Times* – in
plenty of time to send back to London for Sunday evening news pro-
grammes. But by Sunday mid-morning most copies would have been

safely printed and spirited quietly away to Frankfurt airport at the peaceable hour of 4 a.m.

On Saturday morning Mander took out a final piece of insurance. Although the pickets at Tercuman were reported still to be amiable enough, he decided to order a second set of negatives from Gutfreund. The first set of negatives was being sent to Tercuman a page at a time, to be turned into plates as they arrived. A second set of negatives, secreted in Mander's room at the Sheraton, would give him a second opportunity to publish the paper from another printer if things finally went sour at Tercuman.

Hour by hour through Saturday the pickets built up steadily outside the Tercuman plant. Witnesses say they saw the badges of IG Metal, the huge West German metalworkers' union, as well as those of IG Druck being worn by men in the crowd. They also testify to seeing a number of men wearing scarves in Palestinian colours, a common symbol of the German far left, and to observing the distribution of leaflets denouncing the *Times* in the name of the KPD, the German Communist party. When he visited the plant in the morning Mirchandani saw two uniformed policemen, one of whom addressed the crowd and warned it against using any violence to stop the printing of the *Times*. But a girl told him bluntly, and in English, that the *Times* would not be printed by Tercuman all the same.

Still, an event that can plausibly be passed off as a demonstration against capitalism is liable to attract a crowd of sympathisers almost anywhere in the Western world. It was a weekend that ran into the annual May Day holiday, a traditional time for radical protest. And the pickets did not appear to be aggressive. Hostile, perhaps, but not violent. Until after midday on Saturday there seemed to Mander no reason why publication should not go ahead according to his timetable.

At about two o'clock that afternoon, however, the picture began to undergo a seachange, and Mander became seriously worried for the first time. Gebhart Ohnesorge, the lawyer who represented the Hesse newspaper owners' association and had volunteered to act for the Times, came direct from Tercuman's to see Mander at the Sheraton. Ohnesorge said that he had talked to police officers at the plant, who told him they had identified among the pickets men with known records of political violence. It was alarming news, but there was nothing to be done about it except wait and hope.

While they waited, Mander and Ohnesorge toyed with some fantastic options. Perhaps they could lift the printed newspapers from Tercuman by helicopter? Or use tracked vehicles to reach the plant cross-country and not, as the pickets would expect, along the road? Both options were eventually dismissed as impracticable, though not without a shade of regret. Eager as the pickets might be to stop the international *Times*, Mander was equally keen to see it printed.

The Tercuman plant was not designed to withstand an assault. It is neither walled in nor fenced off, but stands four-square at the roadside. Like any newspaper publishing house, it needs plenty of direct access, not only for the staff but also for bulky rolls of newsprint and bundles of printed newspapers. Worse still from a security angle, Tercuman's three-storey building is sited at the end of a cul-de-sac. A few yards beyond where the road comes to a stop lies a railway line, and beyond the railway are trees, behind which, every minute or so, aircraft dip down into Frankfurt airport. Directly behind the building are more trees, another part of the forest from which the Zeppelinheim estate was carved. It would be difficult to transport anything of size or quantity in or out of the Tercuman plant except by the single road, and it would be relatively easy to block off the road by parking cars across it – which was just what the pickets had done by the middle of Saturday afternoon. Lines for a battle were beginning to be marked out. It remained to be seen whether battle would be joined.

The pickets had abandoned Gutfreund to concentrate on Tercuman, perhaps in the mistaken belief that Gutfreund had already finished his part of the work. In fact, more than half the pages were still left to be made up on Friday night, and the staff had to work at breakneck speed through Saturday to get them completed. In the late afternoon the indispensable football results were telephoned through from London, and a few minutes after six the last page negatives were ready. Two members of the Times team, Michael Hamlyn and Patricia Clough, drove with these last two pages – the front and the back – to Tercuman and slipped past the pickets without incident, though Hamlyn became aware, for the first time in his life, of the meaning of the old cliché about how the palms of your hands really can sweat with fear.

To those inside the Tercuman plant, who were waiting for the last pages to be made ready for printing, it seemed that the mood of the pickets outside had changed. They had lit bonfires and were drinking and playing music on drums and guitars. But the carnival atmosphere noticeable earlier in the day had disappeared. This impression might have been the product of their fearful imaginations, but events soon showed it was more than that.

A few minutes before the secret 9 p.m. printing deadline the Turkish foreman and several of his printers came rushing down the stairs into the basement reel room, where reels of newsprint were stored, ready to be fed on rollers up through the ceiling to the presses on the floor above. The men made straight for a steel door in the side wall and wrenched it open. Behind the door lay a recess like a large concrete cupboard, built beneath the pavement that ran along the side of the building nearest to the railway line. The recess was open to the sky above through a steel grille let into the pavement. Inside the recess was a compressor, the machine that was due very shortly to start driving the presses.

When the door was opened, more than just the compressor was revealed. The recess had been stuffed full of newspapers and rags, and they had all been impregnated with petrol. If the presses had been started, it seems certain that there would have been a fire and perhaps an explosion. Luckily, one of Ilicak's staff happened to look out of an upper window at a moment when one of the pickets could be seen pouring something from a can through the grille, and a squad had been sent to investigate. Had the incident not been observed, the consequences of starting the print run might have been fatal.

Ilicak immediately decided that he could not go ahead with printing unless he had much more police protection than the two plain-clothes men inside the building and the two more outside. He called Mander at the Sheraton, and Mander agreed. Ohnesorge, who had by now returned to the Tercuman plant, called the Offenbach chief of police, Kurt Lower, and soon afterwards Lower appeared at the plant in person. Lower asked if the presses ran silently; he was told that the din of printing would certainly be heard outside. Ilicak asked

Lower if he could provide more police. Lower said there were some uniformed men waiting out of sight in the forest behind the plant. But the demonstrators might try to force their way in when they heard the presses running, and if they got inside, they would probably try to smash the machinery. And even if he summoned up enough men to protect the building and to secure the printing of the paper, which he did not think possible, he could not guarantee the safety of the trucks that would ferry the thousands of copies to the airport. Perhaps, Lower suggested, the right thing to do would be to forget about printing tonight and reassess the position in the morning.

Though Ilicak was furious, he decided that he had no choice but to abandon the print run, at least for the time being. When Mander spoke to him soon afterwards, Ilicak was still in a militant mood and even willing to have another try at printing. 'You do not understand,' he told Mander. 'We are Turkish, and the Turks have no fear.' But Mander confirmed Ilicak's decision not to go ahead. The physical safety of the staff – English, German and Turkish – must come first.

Throughout the evening Mander had put up a cheerful public front at his hotel. At 7 p.m. he invited reporters covering the story to the bar for a drink, along with Rees-Mogg and his deputies, Louis Heren and Charles Douglas-Home, all three of whom had flown out the night before for the birth of the international *Times*. Mander's purpose was to display confidence in the success of his project, and his plan would offer the useful bonus of diverting the reporters' attention. If they were not drinking with him, they might be tempted to drive to Zeppelinheim, where, if things had gone to plan, they would have found the paper being printed the night before they had been told to expect it. The reporters found Rees-Mogg in high spirits at the prospect of soon being back in print.

Mander went in to eat with three *Times* journalists and two *Times* technicians who had finished their work at Gutfreund's and had come to the hotel for a celebration dinner. The reporters stayed at their posts by the bar, from where they observed Mander being summoned to take a succession of telephone calls, one after the first course and two more before dinner was over. It was obvious that something was up. Mander invited all the Times staff to join him in his suite for an urgent meeting. There, when Mander took yet another telephone call from the Tercuman plant, John Edwards of the *Daily Mail*, who had briefly joined the group, distinctly heard the strains of the 'Internationale' coming across the line from the triumphant pickets outside the Tercuman building.

Whatever the worth or the wisdom of the project, the *Times* staff in Frankfurt had been caught up in the excitement of getting a paper back on the streets, an excitement that had kept them going through all the peculiar and unusual difficulties of producing the *Times* with unfamiliar equipment in a strange city where most of them could not speak the language. To newspapermen there is nothing quite so frustrating as a missed issue. And that, to the group gathered in Mander's suite, seemed now to be the unavoidable fate of the international *Times*. All the elation of a few hours before had vanished. There was nothing more to be done.

Then Patricia Clough, who had returned to the hotel with Hamlyn, suddenly remembered a contact who might be useful – Ekkehard Greis, the Interior Minister of the Land of Hesse, the man with political responsibility for the police in the Frankfurt area. Perhaps he could do something? She tracked him down at his home and told him, in unambiguous terms, that it was disgraceful that the *Times* had been unable to print in Hesse because of threats of violence. Where did that leave the freedom of the press in Germany? The police had been unable to help – could he? He promised to speak to Lower; and the next morning, when she spoke to him again, Greis assured her that the *Times* could now have all the police protection it wanted.

Later on Sunday morning Lower invited Mander to visit police headquarters in Frankfurt. Around noon a meeting began, with six senior police officers on one side and Mander, Rees-Mogg, Heren, Clough, Ilicak and Ilicak's uncle, who had arrived from Istanbul, on the other. Lower confirmed Greis's promise. He could guarantee that the paper would be printed and distributed in safety that afternoon. Police leave had been cancelled throughout Hesse for the May Day weekend, and he could call on 500 uniformed men, complete with water cannon and whatever else might be needed, to keep the pickets at bay. But that might not be the end of the story. There could be reprisals against either the Tercuman building or members of the Tercuman staff or their families. And if, as he understood to be the case, the *Times* wanted to publish a second issue the next weekend, there could be another picket then, perhaps 1000 or even 10,000 strong.

Mander questioned him. If they printed that afternoon, would people get hurt? Yes, was Lower's answer. Even killed? 'There will be a big fight and it will be bloody,' Lower replied. His answer was imprecise, but it contained enough hints of danger for Mander, Rees-Mogg and Heren. Each of the three independently reached the same conclusion: it would be immoral to risk life and property for the sake of one issue of the *Times*. Ilicak offered to print the paper just the same. It was, he said, a question of honour. And if they could not do it in Frankfurt, then they would do it in Istanbul, where at least the Tercuman plant was secure, or in Kuwait or Lebanon. When Mander declined the offer to print, Ilicak's uncle appeared relieved, though a journalist thought that one of the police officers looked a little disappointed, as if the decision had robbed him of the chance of a good fight.

The *Times* international edition now seemed to have been killed stone-dead. In the early afternoon an IG Druck official announced through a loudhailer to the pickets at the Tercuman plant, 'The *Times* will not be printed here.' The crowd of a hundred or so broke jubilantly into the May Day hymn 'Brothers, to sunshine and freedom'. Then, having been assured by Ilicak that even the 200 copies of the *Times* that had been produced in a test run the night before would be destroyed, the pickets dispersed.

By doing so, they missed the end of the story. Ilicak might have destroyed the copies which had already been printed, but he had not spoiled the plates which printed them. Earlier, at the police station, Heren had asked him if Tercuman might not run off a few copies as souvenirs. Ilicak said he could. But he did more than that. Once the pickets were safely gone, he ran off 10,000 copies. The negatives Mander had kept in reserve were flown that night to a secret destination in the United States, where the newspaper could have been printed in safety. But they were not needed. Tercuman's 10,000 copies were enough to keep the honour of the project intact.

The fate of the international *Times* was eccentric. It was to be seen on sale in the ordinary way at a few places in Holland, Belgium and the United States. (It had never been intended to sell the paper in

Britain.) Individual copies were mailed to people in 120 countries. Clive Lovesy flew to Washington and, enlisting the services of a reliable taxi driver, made sure that one copy was delivered to the White House and another to the British Embassy, where Peter Jay, who had recently been the *Times*'s economic editor, was installed as ambassador. Passengers on a Concorde flight from Washington to London were presented with free copies. It created a brief sensation in the Cabinet Office in Whitehall. The rumour was that it contained some astonishing indiscretion about Britain's defences. But nobody could lay hands on a copy to see if the rumour was true. Rees-Mogg, according to the same network of rumour, had personally sent a copy to the Queen. Perhaps she could be persuaded to lend it to her civil servants? But it did not matter. There were no sensations in the international *Times*. Its greatest impact was through other newspapers and television, which reported the successes of the Tercuman pickets with some relish. Within a few months it had become a collector's item, with a price of £100.

The Frankfurt adventure solved nothing, but it had important repercussions all the same. To the staff who had been caught up in the excitement of getting the paper out, the failure to print the promised 80,000 copies was a plain let-down. But the experience was also a revelation to most of them of what could be achieved with even the simple forms of modern technology used at Gutfreund and Tercuman. These were modest workshops compared with the 'great cathedrals' of Fleet Street – a phrase of Rees-Mogg's – and yet they managed to produce a newspaper which was more accurate and better printed than the *Times* itself had been for years. For Rees-Mogg the inability to print involved a matter of principle. The *Times*, he said in a statement, had been 'in the front line of the issue of the freedom of the press'. He went on, 'I cannot accept that trade unions in Britain, Germany or anywhere else have the right to decide whether people have the right to publish even on a limited basis.'

The *Times* journalists responded to the failure by reversing their decision to co-operate with international publication. Back in London on the Monday, Rees-Mogg told a chapel meeting that the company had no plans to publish another international issue. After he left the meeting the chapel voted not to work on any more such adventures. As had happened the week before with Harold Evans and the *Sunday Times* journalists, Rees-Mogg had made the path of trade union virtue easy for his journalists to tread. Following the trade union line would not any longer mean coming into conflict with the newspaper or the company.

In fact, if Frankfurt had been successful, it might have broken the deadlock, as the company had hoped. During the short period when publication seemed likely, several union leaders made private approaches to the company. For a brief moment it looked to them as though the newspaper might slip away abroad, beyond their reach, and they were suddenly ready to negotiate again. But when Frankfurt went sour, their confidence in their own stand naturally increased. Now, it seemed, their reach extended even to the heart of Europe. How could they be defeated?

Had Frankfurt spurred a breakthrough, the hierarchy of the Thomson Organisation would have been delighted. As it turned out, the Organisation regarded Frankfurt as a mistake, a diversion from the necessary reconciliation with the British unions, something that would only make agreement more difficult. Rightly or wrongly, Denis Hamilton and Gordon Brunton came to believe they had not been kept fully informed, and from then on they decided to become more closely involved in the Times's affairs.

The venture did not quite end with the departure of the Times team from Frankfurt. Ten days later Tercuman staff found a plastic bag near the main entrance to the plant. They called the police, who examined the bag and found that it contained nearly three-quarters of a pound of explosive and an electronic detonator. The bag was packed with flint stones. Only a battery defect prevented it from exploding. If it had gone off, the flints would have scattered with the force of an anti-personnel bomb, killing, police experts reckoned, perhaps a dozen people. Weeks later, Serhat Ilicak's car was machine-gunned by an unidentified gunman. Ilicak emerged unhurt from what may have been an assassination attempt or just a warning.

There was at least this consolation to be found in Gray's Inn Road; bitter as the dispute was, there was no violence there.

8
IN
LIMBO

The shutdown was a weird limbo of a time. On my increasingly rare visits to Gray's Inn Road I watched the life go out of the offices through the windows of New Printing House Square across the street from my room in the *Sunday Times* building. Before Christmas there was a burst of vitality when decorations went up, but after the New Year, when dismissals began, the *Times* offices quickly emptied, leaving only a few posters denouncing the company glued to the window glass. A handful of lights that had been left switched on grew slowly dimmer, until at last they went out. Soon only the lights behind the curtained windows of the directors' rooms on the sixth floor burned regularly into the night.

A few routines were kept going. Rees-Mogg held regular conferences with his senior journalists. The *Times* obituaries were kept up to date and so was a file on events, to help the *Times* maintain its index and its reputation as a newspaper of record. One Saturday I dropped in and found an elderly messenger in solitary possession of the *Sunday Times* offices. He was distributing among empty editors' desks the news agency messages that were still chattering in along the wire. But most ordinary work was impossible: without the spur of real deadlines newspapermen cannot take their jobs very seriously.

Most of the staff who were fired found other work, some better paid, some less so. There was not much material hardship, but there was a very great deal of distress. People who had spent their lives at the newspapers could not understand why the company should dismiss them, especially those who knew they had done nothing to deserve it. The dispute stormed in everybody's mind, like slightly different versions of a melodrama shown in dozens of cinemas at once.

For the journalists it was perhaps especially weird. The first few weeks were quite fun, like a holiday. We could not imagine that the newspapers would be closed for long. But the weeks turned into months, and, unlike others who were still on the payroll (mainly managers and maintenance staff), we had no proper function to perform. We tried some long-term projects, but we lacked conviction, most of all with ourselves. Who, we wondered, wants to talk to a reporter without a newspaper? We felt unhorsed, a little smaller than life. Books were one alternative to newspapers. Bob Ducas, who ran the New York office, flew over and stitched together publishing deals totalling nearly $300,000 for *Sunday Times* journalists who undertook to write books on subjects ranging from the new Polish Pope to the Marseilles Mafia.

We developed our own strategies for survival. Harold Evans, in the time he could find away from the dispute, helped Henry Kissinger with his memoirs. Louis Heren embarked on an account of the condition of Britain. John Whale, a *Sunday Times* writer, produced a book about the parsons of his parish church at Barnes. Jilly Cooper, the columnist, wrote no fewer than five books. Ian Jack, another *Sunday Times* writer, flew to India as soon as the newspaper closed and flew back, reluctantly, four months later with a wife. Bernard Levin also went to India, where he spent some time at an *ashram*. A group of journalists put together a parody *Times* called *Not Yet the Times*, which sold 350,000 copies at 60p and turned them in a handsome profit. Philip Howard, the *Times* literary editor, hired himself out as a jobbing butler. For many, though, the shutdown was a demonstration of the old truth that you will do what you get paid to do – in our case that meant being paid to do nothing. But it was not pleasant to be deprived of the usual rhythms of our lives, which were tuned to the publication of our newspapers. More than one doctor prescribed the end of the dispute as the only remedy for journalists anxious about their state of health.

Like the Blitz, the shutdown became a way of life, and as the weeks and months went by, it turned into an institution with its own forms and rituals. For the camaraderie of the Underground shelter, the *Sunday Times* journalists substituted weekly chapel meetings, where tensions were relieved and wonderful schemes for ending the war were aired. Many (all too many) all-clears were sounded, only to be followed by new siren warnings. Peace, it seemed, was always on the

point of breaking out, which added to the tension. For we were re-
peatedly told to stand ready, only to be told to stand down.

The *Sunday Times* journalists published four issues of the *Sunday
Times Reporter*. Chapels covering most of the company's employees
formed a liaison committee, whose officers included Barry Fitzpatrick, Barry Parsons of the NGA, Jake Ecclestone of the *Times* and
John Fryer of the *Sunday Times*. The committee also spawned a new
title, the *Times Challenger*. The unions organised one meeting at the
Friends' Meeting House in Euston Road, another at TUC headquarters and a third at the YMCA hotel on Tottenham Court Road.

Perhaps, we journalists thought, instead of moping we could do
something useful? If the combined efforts of the unions, the company and the industrial establishment could not dig us out of the
trenches, maybe we could find a way for ourselves. Since the dispute
was raging inside all of us, we each had our own answer. Fire Hussey
and Nisbet-Smith! That was the solution lighted on by the *Sunday
Times* journalists' chapel early in January and eagerly taken up by
all the other chapels. It was a pointless gesture. Even if they had been
the only two responsible for the company's strategy – and they were
not – nothing could have cemented them more securely in their jobs
than chapels calling for their dismissal.

We thought of finding our own mediator. Why not Theodore
Kheel, who had just helped to sort out a newspaper dispute in New
York? He was willing to try, David Blundy, the *Sunday Times* man
in New York, established, if the unions and management wanted
him. But neither did.

What about another political intervention? The orthodox political
magic had failed; the unorthodox might be better. Our first experience, however, was unpromising, almost farcical.

The liaison committee had arranged a public meeting in the basement hall at TUC headquarters at which it hoped to launch a peace
initiative of its own. But the chapel fathers could not agree on what
initiative to launch. The most widely canvassed idea was to offer the
company a guarantee of peace for, say, six months, but some fathers
did not think that they could deliver their chapels, and others did not
want to try. As it happened, the meeting had been fixed for the evening of the day after Albert Booth had persuaded the company and
the union leaders to accept his initiative, so even if the fathers could

have agreed on something, the Booth programme would have up-staged it. That left only one hard item on the agenda, a speech by Tony Benn, the Government's Energy Secretary.

As the Labour Government was disintegrating in a flurry of strikes, Benn seemed increasingly anxious to dissociate himself from its policies, though he was one of the Ministers who shared the collective responsibility of the Cabinet for making them. Benn had already suggested that the *Times* be taken over and run by the BBC, and it was possible that he would use the meeting to distance himself further from the Cabinet by denouncing the Booth plan, which would, of course, puts its fragile prospects even more at risk. Harold Evans called Benn privately and asked him to say nothing that might have that effect. Benn read Evans a lecture on the aspirations of the working man, which he claimed to understand, but he agreed not to dissent from Booth.

But the Prime Minister too was concerned. James Callaghan had no wish to add a public brawl between two of his Ministers to his mountain of troubles. The first hint of Prime Ministerial displeasure reached us when one of Benn's officials rang John Fryer, who was helping to organise the meeting, to warn that Benn would probably not be able to attend that evening. After lunch Benn himself came on the phone. For the first time in his life, he said, he had been instructed not to appear at a meeting. But he had thought of an ingenious wheeze for getting round Callaghan's *diktat*. He would record his speech and send the tape to be played at the meeting.

Fryer, who was himself due to stand as a Labour candidate in the election which must come soon, bravely refused. It was a public meeting, he told Benn, and there had to be a real speaker, not a disembodied voice. Benn responded with another compromise. He would brief one of his close colleagues in Parliament, Brian Sedgemore, to speak in his place, and he would give Fryer the headlines of what he would have said if he had been able to come in person. This conspiratorial prelude whetted our expectations inordinately. If Benn had to go to these lengths to be heard, he must have something pretty sensational to say. But as it turned out, neither Evans nor Callaghan need have worried. He had nothing to say that could upset the Booth plan or even rouse much interest in his audience. To judge by what we heard from Fryer and Sedgemore, Benn's absence was more titillating than his presence would have been.

In May Labour lost the election to the Conservatives, and James Prior replaced Albert Booth as Employment Secretary. A new Government, we hoped, might have some new ideas. Rees-Mogg was among Prior's first visitors. The two men were of an age and they had been at Charterhouse together. But the new Government was ideologically and temperamentally reluctant to involve itself in industrial disputes. Besides, from the start Prior had been sceptical about the Times strategy, thinking of it rather as an enactment of one of Rees-Mogg's gloomier leaders about the state of the nation, requiring strong men and strong measures, as though Rees-Mogg had emerged from his study to make a laboratory experiment of his convictions. Prior kept in touch but held off from taking action. Rees-Mogg was later to show that he thought as little of Prior's strategy as Prior thought of the Times's. Four months after the *Times*'s reappearance, Rees-Mogg published a leader about the union reform Bill which Prior had introduced into Parliament. It said: 'The trouble with Mr Prior – or is it, perhaps, his strength? – is that he does not have a conceptual mind.' Thus was Prior damned with the faintest of praise.

This did not quite exhaust the political possibilities. Both Tory and Labour Governments had toyed with suggestions of a public inquiry into the dispute. Inquiries are one of the traditional means by which Governments try to break the most desperate industrial deadlocks. But in the end both Governments decided against. It was a measure of the helplessness which Ministers felt in the face of the Times shutdown that they did not think it worth attempting an inquiry. But if Government would not do it, perhaps a committee of suitably prestigious MPs might be persuaded to take on the job?

Political journalists on the *Times* and the *Sunday Times* set about using their contacts to test out the idea. They met doubts from every corner, from Parliament and Whitehall, from the unions and the company. Nevertheless, they found one person at least who was enthusiastic – Edward Heath. Heath had been the last Tory Prime Minister, but he had been replaced by Mrs Thatcher after he led his party to defeat in 1974 and he was excluded now from her Government. It would be a consolation to him to solve a problem her Government could not. Early in June a group of us met him at his Westminster office. He seemed eager to get started, was well-briefed, brisk and self-assured. His committee must be adequately high-powered, like himself; he suggested as the other members Merlyn Rees, recently Labour's Home Secretary, and David Steel, the Liberal leader. We were impressed. But although we did not know it, the moment had already passed. Elsewhere momentum was gathering that was, months later, to get the papers started again at last.

Mediation from outside the industry was not the only solution we sought. A new owner might do just as well. The first potential owner the staff thought of was themselves. With general union support, the *Times* journalists' chapel commissioned a study of the prospects for a co-operative which would own and run the newspapers, and a serious report was produced. Though it did not say so openly, the report radiated a clear message : to be viable, the newspapers would have to be trimmed of staff in much the same way as the present management was trying to do. Little more was heard of the co-operative idea.

Sunday Times journalists had another notion. Perhaps we could sell ourselves as a going journalistic concern to another publisher willing to bring out our work under another title. One of us, Lewis Chester, had been working on a book about the takeover of Express Newspapers by the Trafalgar House conglomerate, and he had come to know Jocelyn Stevens, the chief executive who had skilfully survived the change of ownership. Chester rang Stevens to interview him for the *Sunday Times Reporter*. Almost as a joke, Stevens asked why the *Sunday Times* journalists could not run off a new Sunday newspaper for the Express Group; and he followed that up by asking Chester to lunch – a 'long and relatively liquid' event, as Chester described it – at the end of February.

Stevens told Chester that the *Express* had the office space and the printing capacity to publish 500,000 copies of a new Sunday newspaper. Such a venture would be in tune with the thinking of the chairman, Victor Matthews. For one thing, Matthews was trying to solve the same problems of over-manning as the Times, not by cutting staff but by giving the labour force more work to do. That was why he was starting up the new *Star*. For another, Matthews had made something of a speciality of rescuing distressed national institutions. He had already taken over the Cunard Steamship Company and the Ritz Hotel, as well as the *Express* itself. But Matthews was away in the West Indies, and Stevens would have to consult him before he went any further.

From this lunch there developed a typically accidental Fleet Street follow-up. Chester wrote a note about his talk with Stevens and gave copies to the chapel committee; I showed a copy to Michael Jones, our political correspondent; later, in the House of Commons, Jones passed on the gist of it to Gordon Greig of the *Daily Mail*; Greig telephoned his editor, David English; and English called Chester with a hint that the *Mail* too was interested in us.

For a while nothing much happened. No more was heard from the *Express*, though committee members held conspiratorial meetings in pubs with Brian Park, a *Daily Mail* journalist who had become personal assistant to Lord Rothermere, the *Mail*'s proprietor. It was suggested that we might visit Paris, where Rothermere was sitting out a tax exile, following the death of his father.

At the end of April we finally came face to face with a potential publisher, Rothermere, not in Paris but in a suite at the Howard Hotel, overlooking the Thames. Half a dozen of us sat on chairs and beds in a semicircle round Rothermere, who stood looking (to quote from the note I made afterwards) 'the picture of decadent health, as if he had been maturing in wine and sunshine for forty years'. At one point I asked him what sort of proprietor he would make. Laughing hugely, he replied, 'Excellent.' No, I said, what I meant was that while we might not think much of Times Newspapers these days as employers, we liked them as publishers because they did not interfere with our journalism. Rothermere replied that if he had Harold Evans as his editor, he would not interfere either. But he added a chilling qualification: 'The *Daily Mail* is us and me, so to speak. It is our own right arm and leg.' This was just what we did not want to hear, a publisher who would impose his vision of the world on us, in Rothermere's case a vision which was far to the right.

But whatever we thought of him, Rothermere's real interest did not, apparently, lie in publishing a new newspaper based on our collective talents. What he wanted was to buy Times Newspapers complete. Or was it that he simply wanted to make sure we did not go to the *Express*, his family's long-standing rival? We were never quite sure.

Nor was I ever certain that we really wanted to find another publisher. These were desperate days, when any solution was better than none. It was possible, after all, that the newspapers might never reappear under their present management; that the company might cease trading, and we might lose our salary cheques. But what I think most of us wanted was to alarm our own management into believing that it was on the point of losing one of its main assets – us. That might jolt the company into finding a way of publishing the newspapers again, which was all we cared about.

We misled ourselves, however, if we thought we could sell anything as intangible as our talents. There was plenty of interest in the newspapers but, like Lord Rothermere's, it was in buying them lock, stock and barrel. There were, in all, four serious offers to buy, not counting gossip like that which linked a bid with the name of 'Tiny' Rowland, the head of the multi-national company Lonrho, though no formal approach was ever made by him to the company. But Kenneth Thomson never had any intention of selling. In his own phrase, that was something he 'tried not to think about'. But though sale was never a serious possibility, the mere fact that it was known that there were serious bidders helped to prolong the dispute. It gave union confidence an extra boost by suggesting that if agreements could not be reached with the Times management, there was always somebody more amenable waiting to take over the newspapers.

The shutdown of the papers revealed the predatory face of the trade in all sorts of ways, and, in the eyes of Times management, the *Observer* was the chief offender. Soon after the shutdown began, Robert Anderson, head of Atlantic Richfield, the oil company which owned the *Observer*, telephoned Thomson and offered to buy the newspapers there and then. Thomson quickly rejected the offer. But he was dismayed that another newspaper should try to take such advantage of the Times's troubles, even though it was a rival, and the sense of outrage among management mounted as the months went by.

For the *Observer* went further than any other newspaper to exploit the gap left by the closure. Other newspapers like the *Daily* and *Sunday Telegraph*, the *Guardian* and the *Financial Times* printed more copies, but they did not make radical changes, as the *Observer* did by adding two extra sections to its existing two and by calling itself – as if to rub the *Sunday Times*'s nose in its misfortunes – the 'Expanding *Observer*'. We consoled ourselves with the thought that while the *Observer* might have got bigger, it had not got better. (And when the *Sunday Times* was back on sale, the management could hardly conceal its satisfaction when the *Observer* ran into union troubles of its own.)

The *Observer* also played a part in a sequence of events which roused the deepest suspicions among Times management, though its anger this time was directed chiefly against the *Express*. In February it emerged that the *Observer* was going to install the new technology, but in a way that suited the NGA: it did not intend that journalists should use the new keyboards. That concession to the NGA was disturbing enough, but on 21 February worse followed. The *Daily Express* ran a deep headline above a single-column story on its front page: 'Union deal opens new era for *Express*'. The story said that Express Newspapers had also made a deal with the NGA to introduce the new technology, a deal which would give the NGA exclusive rights to the keyboards for five years.

But the *Express* did not stop at a plain announcement. At some length, it quoted Joe Wade as saying that this deal, coming on top of others with the *Mirror* and the *Observer*, showed that the new technology could be introduced without disruption. According to Wade, it 'certainly gives the lie to the story that the NGA are adopting a Luddite attitude or are responsible in any way for the *Times* and the *Sunday Times* ceasing publication'.

Gordon Brunton was the first to learn of the *Express* story when he ran into Jocelyn Stevens in Claridge's Hotel at a dinner of the 30 Club (a dining club of senior people in the media business) even as the first editions of the *Express* containing the story of the deal were being run off. Stevens told Brunton what to expect, and when he heard, Brunton exploded in anger.

The next day the rest of the Times management shared Brunton's anger when they read the *Express* for themselves. At the very least, it was odd that the newspaper should give so much prominence to a story about technicalities of little interest to its readers and so much space in the story to an attack on the Times. It was even odder when they checked and found that though the *Express* had discussed the new technology with manufacturers like Ferranti, it had not yet placed a firm order. If the *Express* went ahead with buying new electronic systems, it would be months, if not years, before they were installed and working. Why, then, had the *Express* made a deal with the NGA now, and why was it trumpeting the deal on its front page?

Soon afterwards two letters fell into the hands of the Times, both addressed to Les Dixon, the NGA president. One, dated 16 January, was from Jimmy Cox, the *Observer*'s production director. The other, dated three weeks later, was from Stevens. The two letters were strangely alike, Stevens's being in large part a copy of Cox's. So exact was the copying that Stevens had contrived to insert a contradiction into his own letter. He wrote of using a piece of equipment, a Laser-comp photosetter, which Cox's letter said the *Observer* intended to use but which an earlier paragraph of Stevens's letter – one of the few that were not repetitions of Cox's wording – showed that the *Express* did not even have on its equipment list. Nine months later – in the same week that the *Times* reappeared – the *Financial Times* carried a brief story which revealed that the *Express* had abandoned its plans for going into the new technology for the foreseeable future.

At the Times all this seemed clear evidence of a willingness among other newspaper managements to do favours for the NGA even though the result was to damage the Times. The *Observer*'s case for playing things the NGA's way was, however, fairly straightforward. Its typesetting equipment was old and needed to be replaced. Manu-facturers were no longer making hot-metal machines, which left the *Observer* little choice but to go for 'cold type'. And it had been plan-ning the change since long before the Times closure. Seen from Gray's Inn Road, the *Observer*'s timing was an embarrassment, but its decision would probably have been the same whatever happened at the Times. The *Observer* may have accelerated its plans so as to provide itself with better typesetting capabilities in time to take ad-vantage of the *Sunday Times*'s absence. But the *Observer* may per-haps be forgiven for learning one lesson from the Times shutdown: that it was unwise to offend the NGA by trying, in one bold leap, to go over to a new system of typesetting in which journalists operated the keyboards.

The *Express*'s behaviour was probably little more than a reflection of Stevens's own style – exuberant, enthusiastic, upbeat, optimistic. He was forever trying to encourage the unions to look upwards and onwards, like himself. There is no time when a Fleet Street management does not need union goodwill, and gestures of goodwill towards the unions are always worth making, especially if they cost nothing. And at that moment the *Express* needed all the goodwill it could get for its new newspaper, the *Star*.

In an industry as competitive as Fleet Street, it would have been asking more than flesh could stand for the Times's competitors to resist taking advantage of the newspapers' long absence. Times Newspapers had not sought help from its rivals. It had struck out on its own, away from the umbrella of the NPA. There was little point in the company's crying 'thief'. In any case, it is doubtful if the rest of the industry did itself any good by trying to move in on the Times's markets. In order to print bigger issues and extra copies, other newspapers had agreed to raise their labour costs, hoping to be able to cut them back again when the *Times* and the *Sunday Times* resumed their share of the market. But the unions were unwilling to accept the cut-backs, as the difficulties at the *Observer* in mid-1980 showed. It may well prove that in exploiting the Times shutdown, other newspapers only succeeded in making their own underlying problems more acute.

All the same, the rest of Fleet Street might have shown less outright glee at Times Newspapers' problems than it did. Competition is one thing; revelling in a competitor's disasters is another. My own favourite example of this unholy delight was a present which John Junor (now Sir John), the editor of the *Sunday Express*, sent to Joe Wade, which took even the NGA leadership somewhat aback. The present was a framed montage of cuttings from Junor's newspaper, of which the centrepiece was a scathing attack on the Times management by Junor himself. It was inscribed: 'Best wishes, John Junor'.

9
BREAKTHROUGH

For a moment Frankfurt had seemed to offer the chance of a break-through. But when that moment passed, the Times management began a sombre reappraisal. It was increasingly obvious that its 'big bang' solution had failed. The strategy had rested on the assumption of an understanding between the company and the union leaders. At best, the understanding had been fragile; now it was clear that the general secretaries could not deliver their members, however much they might want to. There was nothing for it but to explore ways of reaching agreements at new and different levels in the hierarchies of both the Thomson Organisation and the unions.

Two memos written at about the same time showed that the directors were groping towards a new negotiating style. In one Hussey reversed the attitude he had taken a year earlier. Then he had resisted a suggestion that the Organisation should publicly instruct the Times to go for the shutdown policy, thinking that it would undermine his negotiating authority. An instruction from the Organisation would reveal where ultimate management power lay. It would encourage the unions to try to bypass the Times board and make straight for Brunton and Thomson, which they wanted no more than Hussey. Now, however, Hussey thought that the Organisation should enter into the negotiations. And the shift should be made not apologetically, but with an eye to the greatest impact.

'An initiative would now have to be on a different basis,' he dictated, with the Booth failure fresh in his mind. 'Do they want the papers to survive? Put the onus on them. I think it should also be started with different personnel. It ought to be done at the highest possible level, i.e. owners not managers. There needs to be a considerable drama about it: "A last effort".'

For the company, then, the shift of level should be upwards, to Kenneth Thomson, the owner. But for the unions the shift should be downwards, to the shop floor, a move that was foreshadowed in

another memo, a paper on strategy written in early May by Duga.
Nisbet-Smith and Donald Cruickshank.

As the two men saw things, there were still some aspects of the
affair from which management could draw comfort. All the staff
without agreements were now firmly off the payroll, and that fact
had to increase the pressure on the unions to settle. Useful progress
had been made with unions like Slade, Sogat and the Rirma section
of Natsopa. There was no need for the company to dilute its objectives. What it had to do was to alter its 'ground plan'.

To do that, it would need to make a number of significant tactical
changes. First, while the company should continue to devise 'unorthodox' solutions like Frankfurt, such arrangements should be regarded as contingency planning not mainline strategy. Second, if
single keystroking were to be the sole barrier to publication, it should
be 'set aside'. Third, there should be no more grand initiatives of the
Booth type. Instead, the approach should be piecemeal, with separate
negotiating plans being put to each union. Finally, and most significant, the company should abandon its reliance on the union leaders
and direct its attention towards 'where we have established true
power lies – the shop floor'.

These two memos contained all the ingredients that went into the
final series of negotiations: intervention at the highest levels within
the Organisation, represented by Thomson and Brunton; the setting
aside of the single keystroking issue; and real hard bargaining with
shop-floor leaders rather than top union officials. But the memos also
recognised that negotiations were not going to be easy. Nisbet-Smith
and Cruickshank were in no doubt about where the real difficulties
would lie: with the machine and clerical chapels of Natsopa and
with their leaders, Brady and Fitzpatrick, especially Fitzpatrick.

Their memo spoke feelingly of what it called the 'battle to curb
the suffocating power' of clerical chapel officials, who were 'not prepared to accept that their role should be representative'. They refused
to recognise 'the company's right to initiate decisions of any kind
without "full consultation, negotiation and agreement" in virtually
every aspect of the company's operations – a cynical passport to
chapel management'. As for Fitzpatrick: 'The negotiations have
been dominated throughout by the *Sunday Times* FOC [father of the
chapel], whose political ambitions clearly outweigh settlement. His

public posture is to "destroy" TNL [Times Newspapers Ltd] management. It is difficult to accept that any further progress will be made with him.'

In its ill-tempered way, the venom of this language was a tribute to the power of the chapels and their fathers. The directors felt that they could no longer look for solutions in decorous negotiations with union leaders. From now on, answers would have to be sought through a combination of high drama and low bargaining.

The company turned its attention first to the issue of single keystroking.

Keystroking had always seemed to me to be quite distinct from all the other issues in the dispute, because it was really an argument between unions about how to handle a new species of print technology, not a parochial squabble within one company. The unions themselves, I thought, should sort out questions of who-did-what, perhaps through the TUC, one of whose main functions was to settle just this kind of argument. Taking advantage of a professional acquaintance I had with Len Murray, I called on him in January and presented him with a lengthy paper extolling this approach. Murray looked at it warily and put it in his briefcase. Whether or not he read it I never learned. At any rate he did nothing about it.

But I was convinced that it was a good idea and I tried to promote it through the *Sunday Times* journalists' chapel, which passed several motions of support. Still nothing happened. Then in April the idea suddenly took wing, and in June a version of it became part of an agreement which marked the decisive breakthrough in the long deadlock.

It would be gratifying to be able to claim that mine was an original idea and that I was the hero of the settlement, but it would not be true. It was a central characteristic of the Times dispute that it threw up no new ideas and no heroes, only some ordinary people and some thoroughly well-worn notions. Ideas came and went, flowered and died, and the ones which were successful were those which happened to fit when every other idea had been discarded. It was entirely typical that this particular idea was taken up only through a series of accidents.

When in April the *Times* journalists decided not to ban work on the Frankfurt issue, their decision was acutely embarrassing to Jake Ecclestone, their chapel father. The decision was taken in the same week that the NUJ held its annual conference at Ayr and after the union's executive had told the *Times* chapel not to co-operate in the production of a newspaper in Frankfurt. Ecclestone was vice-president of the union that year. He was thus put in the awkward position of being father of a chapel which had decided one thing and vice-president of the union to which the chapel belonged which had decided the opposite.

Seaching for some way to repair the damage, Ecclestone rang New Printing House Square from Ayr and told members of his chapel committee to follow up hints that William Rees-Mogg had seemed to drop about a change in the company's attitude towards keystroking. Committee members met Rees-Mogg, who was accompanied by Hussey and Nisbet-Smith, and they heard that the company was indeed willing to put a new gloss on its demands. Hussey recorded his latest thinking in a three-paragraph letter to Ecclestone, and, after some prompting (mainly from Clifford Longley, the *Times*'s religious affairs correspondent), he included the same three paragraphs in a letter addressed to Les Dixon, which was dispatched by car to the NGA's Bedford headquarters on 2 May.

By this time, however, a week had passed. The Frankfurt episode was over. The *Times* chapel had reversed its earlier decision and was no longer willing to work on a foreign edition. And it had picked up the idea of talks on keystroking with the NGA from the *Sunday Times* journalists. The NGA had accepted an invitation to meet the journalists of both newspapers, and a date had been fixed for 3 May. The two unions were preparing to get into bed together. But when Dixon received Hussey's letter, he slipped out from between the sheets. He cancelled the meeting with the journalists and agreed to meet Hussey the following day instead.

Hussey believed that he had made important concessions to the NGA in his letter. All original keyboarding, he wrote, would be done by the NGA; journalists would have access to the new systems only for editing purposes, and there should be an open-ended review after two and a half years, though the NGA did not need to commit itself to the outcome of the review in advance. But the NGA did not like the reference to journalists' editing. Editing included making corrections, and corrections were a large part of the NGA's normal work. Dixon responded with a quite different solution. He suggested the setting up of a new department, in which journalists and NGA members would work side by side. The journalists would give instructions, and the NGA operators would execute them on the keyboards.

Even when Hussey offered to guarantee, as he had done before, that whatever the journalists did, it would not cost the NGA any jobs, Dixon refused to deviate from the principle that only NGA members should be allowed access to the keyboards. Hussey was exasperated. A few days later he wrote to Bill Keys to complain that the way in which Dixon wanted to operate the new systems was absurd: 'In simple terms, it is like having two girls at an airline booking counter, one taking your request across the counter, the other working the [computer-linked reservations] machine.'

What made the discussion even more frustrating was that the NGA seemed ready to admit that its position was not really tenable. Hussey wrote to Keys:

> The extraordinary thing was that Eric Gregory [an NGA negotiator] said: 'There is no way under which after three years your aspirations will not be achieved.' Dixon said: 'We would accept the new technology as you want it, but not in one swoop.' If they were to give us this type of commitment in public, of course, it would make the whole position much easier because we are not trying to do it in one swoop. We have always wanted it phased in.

But whatever reservations he may have had, Dixon stuck to his refusal to cede the keyboards to anybody but his own members as firmly as ever. This time, though, his final note was a new one. He would now, he told Hussey, start talks with the journalists. The NGA would make a deal with the NUJ, and the company would have to put up with it. To Hussey's protestations that he would accept nothing imposed by the two unions, the meeting was wound up.

As Dixon had promised, talks did take place between the two unions – four sessions of them. Though they did not break down, they petered out. The NGA declined to come to any more meetings. The journalists were never told why, but they deduced that it must be because they did want to use the keyboards themselves; sensing this, the NGA quietly withdrew from contact.

With that, the company felt that every conceivable compromise with the NGA over keystroking had been tried. Times Newspapers was left with no option but to pick up the suggestion made in the memo by Nisbet-Smith and Cruickshank to postpone the whole question until after the newspapers were published again. This option might have been very much a second best, but since it seemed to be unavoidable, the company might as well make the most of it.

Kenneth Thomson was due in London at the end of June to chair his annual shareholders' meeting on the 27th. It was clearly an opportunity to bring into play Hussey's proposal to involve 'owners not managers'. But it was important to make certain that an intervention by Thomson was successful. The drama of an appearance by the real owner of the newspapers must be exploited to the full. If it turned sour, it would only set back the peace process yet again.

No hint of intervention was dropped at the shareholders' meeting, which was presented with the first annual report of the newly created International Thomson Organisation. It was a bizarre event of its kind. Times employees outnumbered the shareholders in the ballroom of the Portman Hotel. Dr Frank Hansford-Miller, the eccentric chairman of the quixotically patriotic English National Party, moved a vote of no confidence in the ITO board. But his criticism was based largely on the fact that the new structure of the Organisation implied overseas control (from Canada), and it attracted only five votes.

Thomson fielded questions with courtesy and aplomb, but he gave nothing away. The nearest to a clue about his intentions emerged from his prepared statement, in which he declared that he had no 'wish' to sell the newspapers. Did that mean he could be forced to sell against his wishes? I thought it might, and so did the *Daily Telegraph*. We were nearer to the truth than we knew. Earlier drafts of Thomson's statement had come close to making some harsh predictions about the future prospects of the company, but in the redrafting process, which was attended by Times directors, the bluntest cautions were deleted. Public threats, some directors thought, might blight the initiative which they were secretly planning.

Even when Lewis Chester, who held shares as well as being a *Sunday Times* writer, spoke up emotionally to ask Thomson to involve himself personally in the negotiations, Thomson blandly rejected the suggestion, claiming modestly that he lacked the charm necessary for the task. Nothing, it seemed, was stirring; scrutinise what was said at the shareholders' meeting as closely as one might, there was no evidence to be found of what the Organisation would do next.

Two days later I had breakfast with Harold Evans. Waiting for him in the garden of his Westminster house, I read in the *Daily Telegraph* that a meeting had been arranged between Thomson and the NGA. The *Telegraph* predicted that the meeting would be held the next week, but when Evans appeared, he told me it had been fixed for that morning at 11. Evans was curiously confident about the outcome. The reason, I later discovered, was that the negotiations had been more or less settled in advance – by Evans himself.

At the same time that Thomson had been talking to his shareholders, Evans had been in Bedford talking to Joe Wade and Les Dixon. Over lunch they had settled on a formula for dealing with the new technology. Under the formula, keystroking would be 'set aside', to be settled after the newspapers were restarted. The settlement, which must be reached inside twelve months, would involve not only the NGA and the company, but the NUJ and Natsopa as well. All four parties would have to give their consent. For the NGA there was satisfaction to be had in postponement; for the company, in the fact that the NGA had agreed to involve other unions as well as the company in the final settlement, which meant that single keystroking was still on the negotiating agenda.

Agreement came quickly that day, as Evans had predicted. Thomson met Wade and Dixon briefly at Stratford Place, leaving the detailed negotiations to Brunton and Hussey. By evening the deal was agreed and announced in a press statement. Thomson had been seen to intervene – lending the necessary touch of drama to a bargain that might otherwise have seemed mundane – but the real breakthrough had come earlier, with the company's willingness to put off the settlement of keystroking until the newspapers were published again and the NGA's willingness to involve other unions and the company in the ultimate solution.

Thomson's participation was not quite over. Other union leaders might want treatment equal to the NGA's – an encounter with the

Times management at the highest level. They did, Owen O'Brien of Natsopa for one. Nothing came of later meetings, but protocol required that Thomson meet other union leaders if that was what they wanted, and Thomson gamely observed the rules.

Keystroking was now almost out of the way, and it should no longer cast its long shadow over all the other issues. All that was left to be done was for Dixon to sell the compromise to the NGA chapels. It was not difficult. The NGA was a more tightly knit union than most, and Dixon had taken special care to keep in touch with the mood of his members at the Times. He had met them most weeks, and he was not likely to make a deal with the company which they would not accept. And so it proved: his compromise was not resisted by his members.

The keystroking agreement had shown that it was possible to reach the shop floor – where Nisbet-Smith and Cruickshank had concluded that union power really lay – through union leaders. With other unions, however, reaching the shop floor would be altogether more tricky.

The broadest, most direct and most obvious route to the shop floor was through the chapels' liaison committee. But the company was still hesitant about giving the committee any recognition. To do so would enhance the authority of the chapel fathers, which was exactly what the company had been trying to diminish; and it might antagonise the union leaders without necessarily conferring any benefits. In line with this view, Hussey and Nisbet-Smith declined an invitation from Barry Fitzpatrick to meet the committee at the end of April.

Two weeks later, however, there was a change of tack. Fathers of the electrical and engineering chapels met Nisbet-Smith and, in the course of discussing something else, again asked him to meet all the chapels together. Nisbet-Smith said there were too many fathers for it to be useful to meet all of them at once; but he would meet a delegation of, say, fourteen. The liaison committee turned that down. The fathers were too jealous of their own standing and of their chapels' sovereign rights to let a few represent them all; it had to be all or none.

Denis Hamilton, who had flirted with the idea of meeting the committee before, decided to accept the challenge. He agreed to meet all the fathers. A date was set, 12 June, and the meeting took place in the Welsh Club, a few yards up Gray's Inn Road from New Printing House Square. What Hamilton heard was mainly a deluge of complaints about the management, but the mood was sufficiently encouraging for him to propose another meeting. He wanted it soon, but it took another month to fix. Fitzpatrick and Parsons were away on holiday, and the committee's organisation was so tenuous that nothing could be arranged without them.

By the time of the second meeting, which was fixed for 4 July, things had moved on. Thomson had intervened, and new technology was no longer the overwhelming issue. That much we all knew. What we did not know was that a good deal more ground than technology had been covered at the meeting between Thomson and the NGA. Although the news for public consumption was that the NGA had agreed only how to handle the question of keystroking, Wade and Dixon had secretly given their approval to a package of proposals for settling all the other issues that stood in the way of restoring the newspapers. Their approval did not amount to a full agreement, but it was enough to encourage Brunton and Hussey to believe that their proposals were worth putting to the other unions.

This posed delicate problems of presentation. The structure of power was different in each union, and, while it might be possible to make deals with the NGA through its leaders, the same procedure was not likely to work with other unions. There was no simple or single way of treating all the unions both equally and effectively, and the company inevitably settled on a compromise. Hamilton would use his meeting on the morning of 4 July to paint a broad-brush picture of the company's proposals for the chapel fathers; and that afternoon Hussey and Nisbet-Smith would lay the details before the union leaders. If both groups gave their approval, then serious negotiations could begin at whatever level was appropriate in each union.

The company's proposals fell into two parts: first, a set of nine 'minimum practical conditions' for restarting the newspapers; and, second, a programme for hiring the staff again once these conditions had been met. The nine points were not comprehensive. There would be plenty of details left to settle once the newspapers were back on the streets. The aim now was speed. The directors' fears for the newspapers' viability had increased. If they were not back soon, they might not be worth bringing back at all. In order to streamline the argument, the company proposed a truce on wages. Staff would come back to work at their old pay rates plus 20 per cent. When the staff were working again, the chapels would be able to negotiate more cash as part of their final agreements with the company.

The Times board fussed and agonised over its proposals, trying desperately hard to make sure that it had pitched them exactly right. Harold Evans, for example, wanted to leave the ninth point out altogether. It dealt with staff reductions, and he was afraid that the unions might throw out the whole package because of it. William Rees-Mogg, however, felt differently; he wanted the ninth point kept in. At a board meeting Hussey listened to the argument, then moved what he pointedly called the 'Rees-Mogg amendment'. The ninth point stayed.

By 4 July the directors had agreed on the proposals which they would put to the unions. Whatever their individual misgivings, they had settled on a common policy. In the act of presentation, however, the policy went adrift.

Armed with a much edited set of speaking notes, Hamilton arrived with Hussey and Nisbet-Smith for his second meeting with the chapel fathers in the upstairs hall of the Holborn public library, a few yards from Gray's Inn Road. It was immediately obvious that the fathers saw Hamilton as an ally and the others as enemies. While the fathers drifted in and the platform party found its seats, the gravelly voice of Roy 'Ginger' Wilson, Reg Brady's deputy, stage-whispered: 'Give it to 'em, CD, give it to 'em, boy.' Hamilton warmed visibly to his reception.

As a bid for reconciliation, his performance was masterly. He embroidered two themes. One was that we were a family of newspapermen who all wanted to be back at work producing our newspapers. He had known many of the faces in his audience for thirty years. Did we not remember how he used to bring his own children to the office when they were only so high? He stretched out his hand to show how small his grown-up children had once been. His other theme was military – he spoke of how you never moved up to the startline without a plan, and how vital communications were in any enterprise. He himself had been briefed for three days before the invasion of Normandy. Wilson chipped in to say that he had only been a gunner in those days, and Hamilton replied, like an old battle comrade, that it must have been Wilson who dropped a few rounds short on him in France.

Throughout all this Hussey and Nisbet-Smith sat silent, growing more and more depressed. For in Hamilton's message of good will the company's policy had become almost entirely obscured by his geniality. He left the fathers with the impression that there was very little to argue about. The staff, he seemed to say, could all come back to work with a handy rise in pay and, for those who had been sacked, a useful bonus of £200. There would have to be a few changes here and there, some pieces of new equipment and some different shift times, but they were trivial matters hardly worth describing as problems. When Hamilton finished I turned to my neighbour and said: 'It's total surrender.' The fathers swelled in triumph. To them it seemed that the company was ready to concede reinstatement for the staff without insisting on the conditions which it had been after all along. The company was surely on the run.

But now Hussey and Nisbet-Smith had to carry the company's message, unadorned, to the Charing Cross Hotel, where they were due to meet the union leaders. By the time they got there, word of the morning meeting had got around. The evening newspapers had printed stories over lunch which made it appear that the company was negotiating with the fathers rather than with the union leaders. The result was that the argument that afternoon turned out not to be so much about the content of the company's proposals as about the way in which they were to be negotiated and at what level within the unions.

The disarray was illustrated by an exchange between Dixon and Ecclestone, who had been at the morning meeting in his role as chapel father and was there in the afternoon as the new president of the NUJ. Arguing over the level at which negotiations should be conducted, Ecclestone said: 'It is a very difficult decision. I really don't know what to say. I don't think the FOCs will be happy at being ruled out.' To which Dixon responded: 'We are not ruling them out. Sir Denis Hamilton . . . should point out to the FOCs that the discussions are now at national level. If we do it any other way, it will create total chaos.'

By now, though, there was likely to be chaos at whatever level negotiations were conducted. A week later the chapel fathers caught up with the company's true message, and they were horried. As they came into the Holborn library to prepare for another encounter with Hamilton, they were handed copies of the precise text that Hussey had given the union leaders the week before. It was not at all what Hamilton had led them to expect, being little more than a condensed version of the very package which they had spent almost a year resisting. Who were they supposed to believe: Hamilton or Hussey? They were in no doubt about whom they wanted to believe. That afternoon, in a conference room at the National Hotel in Bloomsbury, father after father rose to his feet to tell Hamilton that he should take the lead in the company because they had no confidence in Hussey or Nisbet-Smith – who again sat glumly silent.

Both the unions and the company were now speaking with several different voices. Hamilton was not broadcasting the same message as Hussey or Nisbet-Smith, and the chapels were clearly at odds with the union leaders. But at least there was dialogue, confused and cacophonous though it might be, which was better than nothing. So determined was Hamilton to sustain the momentum initiated by Thomson's intervention that he insisted Hussey shut no doors on negotiation. Union leaders too were anxious to keep things moving, and it was one of them, Les Dixon, who picked a path out of the morass.

His solution was to lift the dispute once more to a higher level, above the babble of conflicting voices, and to achieve this he contrived another breakdown in negotiations. On 20 July Hussey took a new version of the company's proposals to show officials of all the unions at the NGA's office a couple of hundred yards away from New Printing House Square. The new version was an attempt to marry the company's ideas with all the objections which the unions had made to them. Hussey had prepared a five-page document, and he intended to go through it carefully, one page at a time. Dixon did not give him the chance, however. He insisted on having all the pages at once. Then he demanded a recess and returned from it indignantly denouncing the company's latest plans. He would no longer negotiate with Times management, he told Hussey; any further talks would have to be over his head.

Dixon came out of the meeting to say some harsh things about the company to waiting reporters. He played up the public differences between the directors for all they were worth, claiming that the attitudes of Hussey and Nisbet-Smith in no way reflected those of Thomson and Hamilton. Other union officials made similar noises. But shortly afterwards Dixon sounded an altogether different note when he called Bill Keys. By then Keys had heard of the breakdown on the radio, and he was worried. Dixon told him not to be. It was not as bad as it sounded, Dixon said, and he asked Keys to intervene with Gordon Brunton. Keys said he would, if the Times directors agreed. Almost as soon as Dixon put the phone down, Hussey came on the line to Keys. Hussey sounded less than optimistic, but he was not as gloomy as he made out. Before the meeting with union officials he had been tipped off to expect a manoeuvre by Dixon designed to bring Brunton back into the negotiations; but it would do no harm to let Keys fear the worst.

Keys and Hussey made a deal. Keys would round up the unions for another meeting if Hussey would persuade Brunton to attend. Hussey kept his side of the bargain that afternoon. At the weekend Keys rang Brunton at home, and the two men made a date to meet on 26 July. Keys took home a pile of papers on the dispute, and over the weekend he roughed out a sketch of an agreement, which he took care to let both sides see before the meeting began.

The company also prepared carefully. It could not afford to speak again with discordant voices. Both Hamilton and Hussey appeared with Brunton, and, to make sure there was no more ambiguity, they spoke with one voice – Brunton's. Talks went on until 2.30 in the morning and started again the following afternoon. By 6.30 p.m. they were over. The result was an agreement, based on Keys's draft, for a return to work.

The directors were content. Although the deal was not as cheap for the company as the one which they had made in private with Dixon and Wade, at the end of the meeting they were sure that they had won from the unions all the concessions noted on a revised list which they had drawn up. Harold Evans, with typical optimism, turned the promise of the agreement into a firm deadline. The

Sunday Times, he decided, would appear again on 2 September, and his journalists began to work to that date.

There was, however, a flaw in the agreement. It had been worked out between the Organisation and the union leaders. But as all experience had shown, the authority of the union leaders was not final. The agreement would have to be endorsed by each union at whatever point in the union structure power lay. In some cases, especially that of Natsopa, this meant the chapels. The speed with which the newspapers could return to print would be determined by the pace of the slowest chapel in the slowest union.

Natsopa quickly, and predictably, emerged as the setter of the slowest pace. Teddy O'Brien, Owen's brother, had warned Brunton that it would not be easy to make the deal stick with his chapels. He was right. The chapel fathers soon found many things to object to in the agreement, beginning with the fact that they had not been involved in making it. They proceeded to consolidate their opposition by putting into reverse the policy they had embraced ever since the shutdown. Up to now they had insisted that the company should take their members back on the terms and conditions, including pay, that had prevailed before the shutdown; once that was done, they had said, they would be ready to negotiate new terms. But now, they declared, the staff would not come back to work until they had negotiated full agreements. The half-way house of the return-to-work deal, with its 20 per cent rise in pay, was not enough. And the fathers capped their stand by agreeing among themselves that no chapel would let its members come back to the company until all the chapels were ready.

The Natsopa fathers justified this reversal on the grounds that many of their members had found good jobs elsewhere and it would be unfair to tempt them back to the Times before their prospects had been straightened out. The company was not impressed, judging this to be no more than a cynical excuse for asserting chapel power over both the company and the union leaders. But the company had no alternative but to play things the way the Natsopa fathers wanted.

It was not only the Times management that was dismayed by the tactics of the Natsopa fathers. As the weeks went by and negotiations between the Natsopa chapels and the company went on at the speed of a slow-motion film, leaders of other unions became increasingly angry. On 10 September print union leaders met to discuss the Times, and since O'Brien could not be there, Keys sent him a letter summing up the views of his colleagues. They failed, he wrote, 'to understand the prevailing situation within Natsopa'. Though the Natsopa executive had endorsed the return-to-work agreement, it had failed to get any response from its chapels, and that failure 'was putting into jeopardy the livelihoods of all unions'.

Keys went on to make a harsh suggestion: 'Surely if all unions and your executive have endorsed the agreement and some people are specifically delaying the restart of the publications, is it not possible to put substitute labour into the company?' Keys was, in effect, inviting O'Brien to connive at breaking his own members' stand by throwing their jobs open to other people. In the trade union book there can be no greater crime than that, and if Keys could hardly have expected O'Brien to do what he suggested, it was a measure of his extreme anger and of the dwindling tolerance of the other print union leaders that he should even have put the proposal forward.

Keys' anger made no impression whatever on the Natsopa chapels, and neither did anybody else's. Rage at the delay as one might, there was nothing to be done. Evans's deadline for restarting the *Sunday Times* came and went, and the Natsopa chapels seemed to be as far from agreement as ever. Brady and Fitzpatrick were free to pace the negotiations as they wished. The reality of shop-floor power made itself vividly clear.

It would be tedious beyond belief to reconstruct the slow evolution from July to October of the deals which the Natsopa chapels made with the company. But the exasperating flavour of those months can perhaps be conveyed by some incidents in which I happened to become involved as a reluctant intermediary.

As I regularly do, I went that autumn to the annual conferences of the TUC and the Labour Party, the first in Blackpool and the second in Brighton. Although there was still no newspaper to write in, it was a way of keeping in touch. On the first day of the TUC conference I ran into Brady and Fitzpatrick, both of whom were there with the Natsopa delegation. Brady told me that he had left word in London that he would be in Blackpool for the week,

available to negotiate if anybody wanted to meet him. Later
Fitzpatrick told me that he too would be available.

Here, I thought, was yet another precious week going to waste,
which could only lengthen the absence of the newspapers. I called
Evans that evening and asked him why management negotiators
could not be sent up to Blackpool. He suggested I talk to Nisbet-
Smith. By the time I reached him, I learned later, there had been a
good deal of telephoning between directors. Nisbet-Smith was reluctant to come to Blackpool, and Hussey agreed; both considered
that such a move would only strengthen Brady's hand. But Brunton
instructed Nisbet-Smith to go. Nisbet-Smith had tried to contact
Brady but had failed. He now asked me to track Brady down.

Next morning I found Brady in the lobby of the Winter Gardens,
where the conference was being held. I told him that Nisbet-Smith
wanted to speak to him. But Brady would not make the telephone
call. It was up to Nisbet-Smith, he said, to make the contact. I said
that that was what he was trying to do, through me, but Brady
insisted that he would not talk to Nisbet-Smith unless Nisbet-Smith
called him. I rang Nisbet-Smith, told him what Brady had said and
left him the conference number so that he could leave a message for
Brady. Nisbet-Smith called the number, but it was not until late
afternoon that Brady rang back. The two men agreed to meet in
Blackpool the next day, and when I spoke to Nisbet-Smith that
evening he asked me to find a room where they could talk.

Because of the TUC conference Blackpool was full of meetings,
but I managed to book a room at the Norbreck Castle Hotel on the
North Shore, a small bare place off the cavernous hall where a few
days before the Miss United Kingdom beauty competition had been
held. It was not much, but it was enough for the four people who
were to meet there. I asked for a bar to be put in and for the room
to be booked in the name of Smith Associates. The NGA delegation
was staying at the same hotel, and a notice in the lobby announcing
the presence of Times Newspapers might create problems.

Nisbet-Smith brought with him Fred Nixson, the company's
industrial relations manager, and Roy Wilson, Brady's deputy, making it two from each side. I met the three men outside the Winter
Gardens, took them in through the security and left them to it as
soon as we had located Brady. Three-quarters of an hour later Brady

appeared at the Winter Gardens' bar. 'It's all over,' he said breezily. 'We gave him a stick of rock and put him on the train to London.' Could this be true? I rang the Norbreck Castle to check, Nisbet-Smith was still there. Nothing had gone wrong. Brady was pulling my leg. But it was not the only false alarm that day. When Brady saw the lunch menu at the Norbreck, he threatened to leave. Only the intercession of the manager, who had something else cooked, seemed to prevent a walkout.

The meeting at Blackpool had its sequel in Brighton in October during the Labour Party conference. This time Donald Cruickshank made the trip to negotiate with Fitzpatrick. At Blackpool Brady had not concealed his glee that a director had travelled to meet him. After Brighton the honours were even.

Blackpool and Brighton were not especially important events in the long trudge towards a settlement between the Natsopa chapels and the company. But they exposed the tensions on both sides. Nisbet-Smith did not want to go to Blackpool because it would be one more concession to the chapel fathers' power. But once he had gone, somebody had to go to Brighton too. The two chapel fathers had to be accorded equal deference. Through dozens of little shifts and expedients like these, the two sides, crab-wise and painfully, learned to accommodate themselves to the realities of power which underlay the differences between them.

In October, at last, the components of a deal fell into a shape, which, if it was not complete, was finished enough for the chapels to consent to their members' return to work. Now, surely, we could start the newspapers again? But no, not yet. From the Natsopa negotiations there spun off a new set of tensions, the most serious of all – so serious that the newspapers were nearly lost.

10
CEASEFIRE

The first three weeks of October were like a journey on a mad roller-coaster which hurtles dizzyingly up in the air and down again along an uncharted track towards a destination that may spell either safety or disaster. To be on board was frightening; just watching made me queasy.

It began with deceptive calm, as Barry Fitzpatrick and Reg Brady stitched together the last pieces of their agreements. But every stitch they made caused more distress to the NGA, and as Natsopa's agreements fell into place the NGA's started to unravel.

The return-to-work agreement was supposed to bring all the staff back to Gray's Inn Road at the same time soon after it was signed by the general secretaries at the end of July. But it was a case of all back or none, and Natsopa's insistence on negotiating agreements chapel by chapel meant that other unions had to wait on it. By the end of August the NGA was becoming fretful at the delay. Why should its members have to stay off the payroll because of Natsopa's pre-varications? The NGA revived the threat it had periodically bran-dished before the company of dispersing its members to other jobs, an alarming prospect because it would strip the company of crafts-men who would be vitally necessary to start the newspapers up again. To pacify the union, Gordon Brunton travelled up to Bedford on 30 August, taking Hamilton and Hussey with him. Between them they persuaded Les Dixon to stick to the terms of the July agreement. But that undertaking did not hold for long.

Less than two weeks later Wade and Dixon came to London and persuaded the same three directors to drop their insistence on the July terms. NGA members could come back to work in a few days, on 16 September, even though Natsopa was still haggling and the newspapers could not be published.

It was a risky concession for the company to make. If the NGA men were taken back on the payroll and the company then failed to persuade Natsopa, Times Newspapers might still have to be wound up – in which case it would cost £10 millions to make the NGA members redundant. For this reason alone Thomson in Toronto was reluctant to agree. On the other hand, the NGA might be able to bring some influence to bear on Natsopa. Wade and Dixon agreed to do what they could to hurry Natsopa up, and on 10 September the company agreed that NGA members could come back to work.

From their meeting with Brunton the NGA leaders went on to the TUC, where they talked over the state of the Times with leaders of the other print unions, except for Owen O'Brien, who could not be there. It was after this discussion that Bill Keys wrote to O'Brien, urging him either to sort out his chapel or to put in substitute labour. But Keys's letter was about as far as union pressure on Natsopa went. If Natsopa's own leaders had little influence on Brady and Fitzpatrick, other union leaders had even less.

NGA men were back on the payroll, but soon that was not enough. They were being paid their old rates, topped up by the 20 per cent rise which was part of the July agreement. But evidence was beginning to emerge from the Natsopa negotiations that Natsopa members were going to get some very fat rises. This struck the NGA with a new horror. For a period at least, until its own chapels had made the same final deals with the company that the Natsopa chapels were edging towards, its ancient craftsmen's advantages over unskilled Natsopa men would be eroded. Nothing could be more offensive to the NGA's sense of its own status in the industry than to have its sacred differentials squeezed. As one union official, Bill Booroff, put it, that would be 'more than flesh and blood could bear'. The NGA did not bear it. Now, it said, it wanted to do the same as Natsopa: to negotiate final agreements, with money to match, before the newspapers were published.

With this, yet another yawning delay loomed before the newspapers. The NGA had just as many points to settle with the company as Natsopa, and it could take just as long to settle them. Even before that could happen, its desire to bargain threatened to upset Natsopa's negotiations, which were still delicate and unfinished. Brady was ready to cut ninety machine assistants from the old shift of 540 men as part of a deal which would give his members £67 for working through Saturday nights. But the NGA machine managers were not ready to do the same. They would, Brady suspected,

demand the maintenance of their old differentials above Natsopa
without making any sacrifice of jobs, which would leave him looking
foolish in the eyes of his own members. At the next to last minute
Brady put in a new claim. His members must be guaranteed 87.5 per
cent of the NGA rate, whatever that turned out to be. In the end he
did not press it, but he had laid down an ominous marker for the
future.

At last, on 4 October, Brady finally signed his agreement, trium-
phantly summoning the press to the Times boardoom, where Harold
Evans and Dugal Nisbet-Smith appeared beside him to listen while
he told the tale of his success. Two days later NGA staff met and
voted to demand that they too must have full agreements before
they would start up the newspapers.

Time, however, was pressing hard. At all levels of the Organisation, from Thomson, through Brunton, to the Times board, it was
the chief concern. Time is money, and in no case more clearly so
than this. The shutdown was costing nearly £2 millions a month,
and the bill had already soared towards £30 millions. But it was not
only a question of money; it was a matter of sheer survival. The
conviction was growing that if the newspapers did not return soon,
they might never return at all. Yet how, after so many months of
delay, was the company to persuade the unions of the sudden overwhelming need for urgency?

The company now decided to build up the pressure in every way
it could. When, on 8 October, the NGA followed up its decision to
re-open negotiations by putting in a pay claim which was far from
modest, the company promptly rejected it. And to underline the
sense of urgency, Hussey asked Dixon to fly back from Stockholm,
where he was at a union conference with Wade, to take charge of
the union side. Dixon did, the next day.

At first the company tried to persuade Dixon to stick to the July
agreement. A letter, signed by both Hamilton and Hussey, went to
Dixon on 10 October, saying that the company was 'in sympathy'
with the NGA on differentials but asking Dixon to sign a reaffirmation
of the July agreement all the same and carefully adding that the
future of the newspapers was 'balanced on a knife edge'. Dixon was
ready to respond to the hint about differentials. He drafted a reply
which said that he would reaffirm the July agreement because of the

company's sympathetic line, but the draft was rejected by his chapel fathers, and the letter Dixon actually sent was altogether tougher in tone. It accused Hamilton of causing all the trouble by agreeing to negotiate with Natsopa and Hussey of breaking a pledge not to let differentials be eroded. But Dixon left a door open by promising to 'proceed with all speed' in negotiation.

On 12 October the company responded. With the aim of getting agreements within a week, management negotiating teams would be made available immediately. The offer came from Hamilton and Hussey, and their urgency was doubly underscored by statements issued simultaneously in London by Brunton and in Toronto by Thomson. Brunton said the consequence of failure in negotiations would be 'the certainty of the losses of thousands of jobs within the company and possibly elsewhere too'; and he added: 'We have no intention of selling the titles.' Thomson's statement endorsed Brunton's, with a warning hint of his own: 'the point of decision is but a few days away.'

Talks opened at New Printing House Square on Sunday, 14 October, and as they went on, management deliberately stepped up the pressure of persuasion so as to remove any lingering doubts that this week was positively the last chance to save the newspapers and the jobs which they provided. On the Monday company executives visited the Departments of Trade and Employment to warn Government officials that there might soon be a final closure and several thousand new names on the unemployment register. On the Tuesday Hussey wrote to the print union general secretaries asking them to be prepared to meet him at 3 p.m. on the Friday. If Wednesday brought no deal with the NGA, he said, then the boards of Times Newspapers and of Thomson British Holdings would spend Thursday deciding precisely what to do, and their decision would be conveyed to the union leaders the next day.

Wednesday, 17 October, was now clearly marked out as the crucial day for the negotiations, and the tensions on that day were almost unbearable. Three of the Times external directors were known to have been summoned back from the United States for Thursday's board meeting, and Thomson himself was flying in from Toronto to take the chair. The fate of two great newspapers and thousands of jobs depended on the NGA's ability to make a deal.

This time there would be no appeal. The smell of death was keen, and reporters and television cameras crowded the hall of New Printing House Square to record the kill.

Though there had been some progress on the issues that divided the NGA and the company over the past two weeks, not one of the fourteen separate deals which the union had to make was within sight by the Wednesday. The NGA had not been granted the same two months as Natsopa in which to argue at leisure the finer points of its dissent with the company, and its negotiators could not crush their arguments into the time that was left. Under the pressure of the deadline the NGA began to crumble.

By Wednesday evening it was becoming obvious to both sides that there was not going to be agreement that night. While Hussey began planning discreetly for the failure he now foresaw, Dixon staged a theatrical crisis in the hall below. Timing his appearance precisely, Dixon emerged from a lift and made straight for Prakash Mirchandani, the BBC reporter who had stayed with the Times story from the start. On cue, Dixon fired a tremendous blast into the camera which went straight out on the nine o'clock news. He had made the company very generous offers, he said, the best anywhere in Fleet Street, and it now had half an hour in which to give him an answer, or that was it – finish. He was visibly charged with emotion. When the television cameras stopped, reporters crowded in, and when I asked him a question about the number of hours that were to be worked in the machine room, which seemed to be one of the issues, he snapped back: 'Don't you talk, Eric. You don't work even four hours a day.' I almost retorted, 'That's because there's no *Sunday Times* for me to work on,' but then I thought better of it. Shortly afterwards, in the Blue Lion pub, Dixon apologised. He had not meant it, he said; he had been up-tight. And he told other reporters that his television performance had been play-acting, a bit of a spoof.

Dixon's half-hour deadline came as a surprise to the directors watching the news on the sixth floor. He had said nothing about it to them before he took the lift down to the hall. But his display was more a way of dramatising the crisis than a real threat.

The Dixon deadline passed, but the talks dragged on. Around one in the morning Hussey decided it was time to bring matters to a head. So far most of the arguments had been about the company's demands for working conditions like hours, shifts and manning. Money had hardly been discussed. Now, Hussey thought, was the time to set his offers against his demands. Perhaps they could then get down to some serious horse-trading – though that was unlikely.

Nisbet-Smith began to read out the company's pay proposals. He reached the second paragraph, which set the first of the NGA rates at £204 a week, but no sooner had he read out the figure than Dixon rose to walk out. Bill Booroff, the NGA's next senior official present, made signs that he wanted to stay to hear more, but Dixon told him to come with him. They left the room together. A few minutes later Booroff came back with two other officials to see if they could start again. But Hussey did not encourage him. He was sure that talks would get nowhere that night. Either they could try again another day or the axe would fall on the newspapers. Booroff burst into tears.

In the hall below reporters received a series of puzzling signals in the early hours of the morning. Denis Hamilton passed through, and when a reporter asked him why he was going home at this crucial hour, Hamilton made a characteristic reply: 'Commanding officers must have some sleep to avoid taking wrong decisions.' And then he added, ominously: 'Some hard and painful ones may have to be made.'

Hamilton was soon followed by Dixon. 'We've broken down, lads. We've had enough of it,' he said. 'Yes, it could be the end of the *Times*.' He made much of the £204 offer he had just heard from Nisbet-Smith, contrasting it bitterly with the £207 that had been offered to a group of Natsopa staff. Dixon rounded on a reporter who asked if he was happy about the breakdown. 'Don't put bloody questions to me like that. I'm not bloody happy to see it close.' Then he left, followed by a trickle of woebegone NGA negotiators.

Half an hour later Mike Mander appeared with William Rees-Mogg to give the company's view. Mander stated icily that what Dixon had rejected as derisory was in fact an offer of £10,600 a year, rising to over £11,000, for a thirty-four-hour, four-day week, with six weeks annual holiday. Pretty good, his taut appearance implied, by anybody's standards. A reporter asked Rees-Mogg if he thought he had edited his last issue of the *Times*. Rees-Mogg thought about the question for a full twenty seconds before he gave his answer: 'No.' It was not the answer but the long pause that stayed in my mind.

If Dixon had waited to hear more from Nisbet-Smith, he would have learned that the one offer he had listened to was not as poor as it had sounded to him. The NGA's £204 was not really comparable with Natsopa's £207. The £204 was for thirty-four hours' work, mainly during the day; the £207 was for forty-five and a half hours' work, mainly at night. It did not destroy the unions' hallowed differentials. But Dixon did not stay. And Hussey did not want him to.

Hussey and Dixon were now sure they were not going to reach agreement that night, and for both men it made more sense to have a clean break, then try to start again, rather than let the talks rumble on acrimoniously through the night to a hopeless impasse at dawn. Both had kept in touch with Bill Keys throughout the day, Hussey calling Keys as many as ten times with the latest news. Keys was at the TUC on business, and when he had finished, he stayed on, helping the caretaker to lock up rather than risk missing something by catching the train home to the Essex coast. He took his last call from Hussey soon after 9 p.m., when Hussey warned that the end was near – for that night at least.

As the likelihood of a breakdown increased through the long Wednesday talks, Keys and Hussey had toyed with the idea that the next thing to do would be to bring the other union leaders back into the negotiations. Keys had quietly passed word to them that they might be needed the following day. They were eager to help, for reasons that spread far beyond the Times and their members in its newspapers. If the *Sunday Times* closed, Sun Printers at Watford would lose the valuable contract it had to print the colour magazine. Sun Printers were an important component of the British Printing Corporation, and the loss of the *Sunday Times* contract could have a ripple effect throughout the whole Corporation, threatening the jobs of many thousands of print trade unionists who had no connection whatever with the Times. The loss of jobs at Gray's Inn Road would be serious; the loss elsewhere could be catastrophic.

Soon after eight next morning, Thursday, Keys rang Hussey at home and told him that he would like to meet the Thomson board before it took any decisions. Hussey said it was not up to him to agree, but he would call Brunton. He gave Brunton Keys's message, and Brunton passed a message back, asking Keys to call him at his office later in the morning. When Keys rang Stratford Place he spoke to another director, James Evans, as well as to Brunton. Both men seemed discouraging. Brunton would not refuse to meet Keys if that was what he wanted, but on the other hand he saw little point in doing so. When Keys put the phone down, he was convinced that the decision to close the newspapers and fire the production staff had already been taken.

Officially, Thursday was the day of decision, when the boards disappeared behind the closed doors of Stratford Place to make their final dispositions under the eye of Kenneth Thomson. That was the story that was repeated to me when I dropped in there to see what was happening in the late afternoon. Michael Cudlipp, a former *Times* journalist who now handled the Organisation's public relations, insisted that there would be no news until Hussey met the general secretaries next day. Tired, I was grateful for an excuse to go home. Prakash Mirchandani, however, was more sceptical of the official line. He hung on outside the building until three carloads of directors emerged and set off at speed. He chased them until they came to a stop at the TUC. When he reported on the nine o'clock news that talks were on again inside the TUC headquarters, I put my shoes on and drove wearily back to Bloomsbury.

With Thomson's approval, Brunton had agreed to meet the union leaders once more. Keys had chosen the TUC for the meeting. It had the advantage that it did not sell alcohol or keep much on the premises. The reports which Keys had heard of the night before suggested that drink played its part in muddling the negotiations, and he did not want that to happen again. There was too much to lose.

Keys spent an hour alone with the union leaders and then a second hour with the directors. What he wanted, he told them, was another extension of the deadline for two or perhaps three days. Brunton was in no hurry to agree. To Keys the directors seemed divided. James Evans, he thought, was the leading hawk, the one most reluctant to agree to any extension at all. There was some truth in his perception. But the apparent divisions between directors also served a purpose. They lengthened the meeting, which suited the spacious negotiating style of the print unions. And when Brunton eventually agreed that the NGA could have until 4 p.m. on Sunday to make agreements with the company, the union leaders believed that the extension was a compromise between the directors and a grudging concession to them. They were in no doubt that when Brunton said he wanted the agreement of all the chapels, as well as of union officials, by the new Sunday deadline, he would close down the newspapers if he did not get it.

On Friday, as the final, final round of talks with the NGA got under way, Hussey pieced together the last details of the company's strategy for the benefit of the union leaders. From the board he went to the meeting he had fixed three days before and told the general secretaries that if the NGA did not make agreements by the Sunday deadline, some 3200 production staff – the entire memberships of Sogat, Slade, Natsopa and the NGA – would be fired for good. Managers, journalists and maintenance men would be kept on while new ways of publishing the newspapers were worked out – perhaps, it was hinted, abroad once more, this time well beyond the reach of the Fleet Street unions. (In fact, a secure arrangement had already been made to print the *Times* in America.) There was no question, he insisted, of the newspapers being sold.

Everything the company could think of had now been done to leave nobody with any lingering doubt that this time there would be no appeal beyond Sunday afternoon. And the union leaders were persuaded. The question that remained was whether the fathers and the chapel members could also be persuaded in the forty-eight hours that were left.

There was no mistaking the different atmosphere when the talks resumed on the Friday. The negotiators were now intense, serious, sober. Strong drink was banished from the offices and dining-rooms of New Printing House Square's sixth and seventh floors. Whatever the outcome, the negotiators wanted to be sure that it was clear and that their judgements were unclouded. Beer was the most that could be had.

Friday brought progress at several points, in the foundry, in telecommunications and especially in the composing room. But when the meetings started up again at 9.30 on Saturday morning, not one of the fourteen necessary agreements had been settled. And settlement seemed no nearer even when Hussey returned to the office after taking a supper break that evening.

Hussey and Dixon held a brief meeting in Hussey's office. It was time, Dixon said, to get down to the bedrock issue of money. They must trade concessions by the NGA against hard cash from the company. Hussey agreed. He also made a decision which he was later to think of as the best he took that weekend. Dispersed as they were in separate groups around the seventh floor, the negotiations had lacked coherence. They must be brought together and put in one man's charge. Hussey decided that Nisbet-Smith should be the man. Nisbet-Smith would, Hussey thought, do the job better than he could himself. He turned his sixth-floor office over to Nisbet-Smith and went down the corridor to join the other directors for the final wait.

Around one o'clock on Sunday morning Nisbet-Smith took stock. As he saw it, he was faced with two fundamental problems. There had been no agreement on money; and the machine chapels were refusing to budge on jobs. He asked Dixon to join him, and alone they concocted a desperate strategy. They would handle the bargaining between them, taking each department in turn and bringing in senior officials from either side but no chapel fathers. Any agreements made this way, Dixon promised, he would ensure the chapels accepted. Nisbet-Smith added a wrinkle of his own. There was no time left for speeches. No sentence that anybody uttered should be more than seven words long.

They began with the composing room.

The sixth floor seemed peaceful enough when I took the lift up there in the early hours of the morning. I had had a drink with Dixon at seven the evening before in the Calthorpe Arms – the Blue Lion had taken to closing on Saturday nights for lack of *Sunday Times* customers – and he had told me to expect a result around 4 a.m. Taking his tip, I had gone home and then returned to see what was happening. James Evans and William Rees-Mogg were passing the time with a handful of managers in a desultory, waiting-room way. They could – or would – tell me nothing. Evans proposed a breath of fresh air. Rees-Mogg, he and I set out on a long, slow tour of Bloomsbury streets and squares, peaceful and quiet at this hour, sharp but cold. As we drew near to New Printing House Square again, Evans interrupted the conversation to ask if I would mind very much not returning to the sixth floor. There would be a lot of tension about, he said, and the presence of a reporter would not help. He was polite, even apologetic, but he meant what he said. Evidently the calm I had thought I sensed was deceptive.

By 2 a.m. Nisbet-Smith had made a deal with the composing room. Two hours later he had a deal with the foundry. Taking a break after that, he met a telecommunications official and tried to make a quick deal with him in the corridor. The official would not bite then, but Nisbet-Smith got his deal by 7 a.m. That left the machine room.

From the start the machine room chapels had been the toughest nuts of all on one issue: jobs. Every other chapel that had been asked had made some concession to the company. But the NGA machine managers had consistently refused. And they still refused. No great numbers were involved: they could be counted on the fingers of one hand. The savings to the company would be slight, hardly worth bothering about for their own sake. The important thing was to show that the NGA was willing to sacrifice jobs in the machine room on the same scale as Natsopa. Argue as he might, though, Nisbet-Smith was unable to move machine officials one inch.

Exhausted and close to despair, Nisbet-Smith took a flier. Were the NGA officials really serious when they said that every single man in the machine room was necessary? Or were they just upholding some branch policy of refusing to give up a single job in any Fleet Street office? If they were serious, why not put their case to the test of work-study? Let the company and the union each nominate three people to an inquiry team, and let them both agree on an independent chairman whom they could trust with a casting vote. In a word, let there be arbitration.

From the three NGA regional officials who were there the first response to Nisbet-Smith was a flat 'no'. But Dixon perked up. Say that again, he requested, and Nisbet-Smith did. Dixon asked him to leave the room, and Nisbet-Smith walked down the corridor to tell the surviving directors of his off-the-cuff idea. When he returned to

Hussey's office, Dixon told him the NGA would accept arbitration after all. But now it was Nisbet-Smith's turn to be discouraging. He had to report that his soundings among the directors showed little support for arbitration. They wanted a full and final agreement on the spot, and Nisbet-Smith appealed to the union officials to make it. The machine room chapels were the only group left in the whole company without a deal. On their decision depended the existence of the newspapers and the jobs of thousands of people. How would they feel if they alone were responsible for cutting off both?

To his dismay, they replied that they would feel fine, even proud. According to one NGA official, they would be received as heroes by their branch if they did not surrender to the Times. The appeal to sentiment evidently cut no ice with this branch of the NGA. Nisbet-Smith was convinced that he had no option but to return to the directors and to try once more to persuade them.

Meanwhile, along the corridor, James Evans was drawing up a list of the pros and cons of arbitration; the number of cons he jotted down far exceeded the number of pros. Even after he and Hussey had talked it over with Dixon, they were still opposed. So were most of the other directors and the twenty or more managers who had been there through the night, some helping in the negotiations, others merely anxious. The overwhelming weight of management opinion was clearly against Nisbet-Smith. It wanted no loose ends left by one set of chapels over which other chapels might trip. There were fears too of what an investigation might throw up. Expert studies had shown that the noise levels, while not out of the way by Fleet Street standards, verged on the unlawful. An inquiry might even show that the NGA claim for more men was justified on grounds of health. Besides, the pressure on the NGA was intense. The general secretaries of all the print unions were due at New Printing House Square at four o'clock that afternoon. Surely the NGA could not hold out until then?

By now it was after 8 a.m. The directors agreed that they should not make the final decision on their own. Brunton must be brought in. He was rung at home, and the directors gathered round a conference telephone to give their views. One by one they spoke – Hussey, Mander, Nisbet-Smith, Rees-Mogg, Cruickshank, James Evans – and they were all against Nisbet-Smith, apart from Rees-

Mogg, who spoke up strongly in his support. Nisbet-Smith argued that it was a breakthrough to get the NGA to agree to arbitration at all. It had refused to go to arbitration over the new technology in April, but now it was willing to let the head of Acas be their judge. In any case, there was no choice. He was sure he could get no deal out of the union that morning. Arbitration was all that was left.

Brunton listened to them all and then pronounced his verdict. He agreed with Nisbet-Smith and Rees-Mogg. Nobody had offered a convincing alternative. Arbitration might not be perfect, but it was better than losing the newspapers. And with Brunton's decision it was over. The last section of the last union had finally been slotted into place.

Camped in the hall below, reporters and cameramen hung about, tired and unshaven, pacing the floor or trying to snatch some sleep, sprawled out on the waiting-room furniture. Before dawn a whimsical touch of colour was added by the appearance of Ivor Spencer, England's leading toastmaster, complete with his red dinner coat, whom Harold Evans had asked to come along and propose a toast to the return of the newspapers. But we still did not know if that would be the right toast. There was a brief stir of expectation around eight when Mirchandani returned. Dixon, he said, had called him at home an hour before to warn him that if he wanted to be present for the result he had better get out of bed. Eight o'clock passed, and another hour, and another, but it was not until a few minutes past eleven that Dixon and Hussey emerged together from the lift. They were all smiles. Ivor Spencer duly popped his cork.

Throughout the morning the NGA chapels met to vote on the agreements that their officials had made overnight. The directors held a celebration lunch with the union leaders while they waited for the results to come in. One after the other these were announced, in each case an endorsement. Shortly after three there was a last rumble of discord. The directors had been especially anxious to make sure that managers who were also union members should not be punished by their unions for coming to work while other union members were out, sacked. Wade and Dixon had made a verbal promise, but the company wanted it in writing. At first the two union leaders refused, but after they had closeted themselves in a room for a few minutes, they emerged with their signatures on the company's document.

With only minutes to go before Brunton's 4 p.m. deadline, everything had been settled. Almost eleven months after the newspapers had closed there was at last no disagreement between the company and any union which need prevent the papers from being published. The *Times* and the *Sunday Times* were saved.

AFTERMATH

The *Sunday Times* published its first issue for nearly a year on 18 November, six days after the *Times* came back into print. There had been a weekend of dread that the *Times* would miss its return because of a row between the NGA and Natsopa over which of them should control buttons on the new counter-stackers. But Bill Keys had superintended a last-minute compromise, and the newspaper was printed. In the *Sunday Times* composing room there was a mood of elation. It had been a bitter fight, but now there was a ceasefire, and it was time to swarm out of the trenches. The tableau of confrontation I had witnessed the last time the paper was printed had quite vanished. Managers and union members mixed; champagne flowed; it was good to be back. In this ambiguous atmosphere, compounded of uncertainty and good will, the newspapers returned to life.

Four months later, on 14 March 1980, a bevy of directors met the company's fathers in a conference room at the Royal National Hotel in Bloomsbury. The informal arrangements expressed the new mood. There was to be a breaking down of old barriers, an end to warfare. The directors – Hamilton, Hussey, Mander, Nisbet-Smith and Cruickshank – occupied one wing of the platform; the fathers – Fitzpatrick, Parsons and Ecclestone – the other. Hamilton and Fitzpatrick took it in turns to be chairman. At tables in front of them, in no special order, sat a mixture of managers and fathers. Consultation was to replace aggression, and this meeting was a gingerly start.

The news that day was in some ways reassuring. Mander reported that both the *Times* and the *Sunday Times* were selling 40,000 copies more than before they shut down. All but one of the company's five titles were selling better than ever, and the drop in the sales of the exception, the *Times Educational Supplement*, could perhaps be explained by the cold winds that were blowing through the education system, fanned by cuts in Government spending. We had been afraid that our newspapers would be forgotten, but it seemed we need not have worried.

News of production was less cheerful. The *Sunday Times* had printed its full quota of copies for only ten of the seventeen issues published since November. And not once had production been good enough to make all the edition changes the newspapers should have had. He did not, Hamilton said, want to read the Scottish football results in the newspaper delivered to his country home at Chichester on Sunday mornings.

There were plausible reasons for the poor production. Presses were old, and they had deteriorated during the shutdown. Not all the old production staff had returned and the new men still did not know their way around. These problems would no doubt sort themselves out in time. More alarming to Hamilton, over a hundred new claims had been lodged by the chapels since November, and dozens more were said to be in the pipeline, in spite of the fact that all the chapels had made agreements that were supposed to last for a year. But at least, according to Hamilton, the new arrangements for handling disputes peacefully had worked. None of the claims had boiled over into a strike or any other kind of overt militancy.

Next day, a Saturday, one claim did erupt. It was a claim by Brady's chapel for 87.5 per cent of the NGA rate, which Brady had raised but not pressed in October. The chapel did not strike. It 'withdrew its co-operation', which achieved the same effect without costing chapel members any pay. 'That and that alone led to the loss of copies,' Brady said in a statement, to which he added defiantly: 'Let management manage, like they did for eleven months, without us.' That night the *Sunday Times* lost 443,000 copies, almost a third of its total print.

Now, suddenly, unrest and disruption were loosed again. The appearance of smooth relations had been deceptive. All the old tensions were still there, lurking beneath the surface. If one chapel could threaten production, so could all sixty-five. Any one of those claims lodged since November could be the cause. We were back to living dangerously again. From then on we found ourselves wondering each Saturday night when – or if – there would be a newspaper for us to take home, and on most Sunday mornings the print run ended incomplete. Wildcat disruptions were what had led the company to its shutdown strategy two years before. After all the agony of the time since then, had nothing changed?

There is no single calculus by which to measure the shutdown. To a journalist like myself it was simply an outrage. We had no quarrel with anybody; our careers were shortened by a year; it was a gross offence against the idea of a free press, since total silence is the severest form of censorship. For other members of staff it was also an outrage, though perhaps of a different kind. Many had been with the newspapers all their working lives. They thought of themselves as Times men and women, and the experience of being dismissed seemed likely to leave permanent scars. They would never feel the same about their company again.

These are intangibles, powerful enough but impossible to quantify. A few days after the newspapers started up again the company attempted a more exact reckoning. Donald Cruickshank calculated the costs and benefits of the shutdown in a memo for the Organisation which was to be the most authoritative verdict on the material outcome of the dispute.

From the day the newspaper closed on 30 November 1978 to the end of 1979, according to Cruickshank, the total cost to the company had been £46 millions. This was made up mainly of the £33.4 millions that the company had paid out in wages and other bills while the newspapers were off the streets and no revenue was coming in from sales or advertisements. To that he added £3.5 millions as the cost of the final return-to-work settlement, including the sums of £500 which had been paid to everybody who had been dismissed; £1 million for the publicity campaign to relaunch the newspapers; and £8.1 millions for the last two months of 1979, during most of which the newspapers were published but, because of a shortage of tele-ad girls, potential advertisement revenue had not been fully realised.

For this gigantic expenditure there could be no adequate return. Commercially, the shutdown could not be justified, and Cruickshank made no attempt to do so. The International Thomson Organisation, however, took its loss with equanimity. Its accounts for 1979 showed that though it had lost £39.3 millions on the shutdown that year, its trading profit rose all the same, from £146.5 millions to £172 millions.

There were other consolations. The new agreements with the unions should bring some savings. There would eventually be 15 per cent fewer people on the payroll. Overtime would virtually dis-

appear. The presses would be run faster to produce more copies
every hour. The *Sunday Times* would be able to print eighty-page
newspapers, eight pages more than previous agreements had allowed.
Shifts had been reorganised so that they meshed properly with the
production timetable. New equipment would be worked, including
a commercial computer and the counter-stackers, which would speed
newspapers from the presses through the publishing room and out
on to the streets. And the most important piece of new machinery,
the electronic typesetting system, would go into limited operation,
with one new composing room replacing the two old hot-metal
composing rooms of the *Times* and the *Sunday Times*.

With fewer people on the payroll and a 10 per cent increase in
output from those who were left, Cruickshank estimated the overall
benefit to the company as a 30 per cent increase in productivity.
For any company this would be a gain worth having, but the Times
had hoped to get an improvement of 40 or 45 per cent. Where was
the shortfall? Cruickshank was in no doubt that it arose from the
casual workers in the machine room and the publishing department.
His judgement was bleak. 'The attack on gross overmanning and
corrupt working practices foundered on an ultimate indifference to
the company and its titles and on the severe lack of sanctions that
the company has over the behaviour and motivation of most who
work in the areas.' Put more crudely, casual workers did not care a
hoot about the company, and there was nothing whatever the company could do about it.

The company had not got what it wanted out of the shutdown;
but was its loss the staff's gain? In Cruickshank's view, it was not.
True, the company's wage costs had risen by 55 per cent. But the
actual wage rates, the money paid to individuals for every hour they
worked, were 'probably no higher than they might have been' without the dispute. Cruickshank believed the company would have had
to make moves towards catching up with general Fleet Street wage
levels whether there had been a shutdown or not. In paying new
and higher rates it was bowing to the inevitable. Even so, in some
(and perhaps most) areas pay had not reached the heights the company itself had proposed. In June Denis Hamilton had promised the
chapel fathers that the company's aim was to put its staff in the
upper quartile of Fleet Street pay. But, according to Cruickshank,

the rates negotiated for many of the Times staff still fell below that level.

Nobody emerged a winner from Cruickshank's account. The staff might have gained its pay rises and the company half or at least a third of its savings in manpower without all the hassle and distress of the last year. But Cruickshank's memo was not the whole story. Gloomy reading though it made, it was in a sense an idealised picture – a kind of snapshot of things as they looked on the day it was written, 21 November, rather than of things as they actually were. For instance, only half the manpower cuts had yet been made. The rest were still to come, and whether they did come or not would depend on further co-operation on the part of the unions and chapels. Cruickshank's sums assumed, among other things, that there would be an easy transition from the two hot-metal composing rooms to a single electronic composing room. But would the transition be easy?

Reaching agreements with the chapels was only the first step for the company. The second step, and the crucial test, was making the agreements stick. If they did not, then Cruickshank's snapshot would become the first frame of a moving picture in which the idealised scene he depicted would be rapidly transformed. The agreements were not legal documents, only a statement of the position the two sides had reached when they left off negotiating. The agreements were liable to challenge at any time, and, in the Fleet Street way, challenges could be expected soon.

Sure enough, they came. In spite of its agreements with the company not to victimise its supervisor members who had stayed at work through the shutdown, the NGA decided to expel some and fine others £1000. Without union cards it would be almost impossible for them to find work anywhere in the print trade; and £1000 was a lot of money. Between them, these measures surely amounted to victimisation. At Bedford Wade and Dixon told James Evans, Hussey and Nisbet-Smith that that was the NGA's decision, and the company would just have to put up with it. But the company decided to go to law. After a brief court appearance and an adjournment, the union executive held an all-day meeting at Bedford, attended by legal advisers. That night, a Saturday, Wade spoke to Hussey and told him the NGA was ready to settle for a milder penalty – a £70 fine.

The supervisors were content to pay, but the legal setback seemed to the company to have profoundly soured the union's attitude towards it.

After that foray there was the challenge from Brady's chapel. And that was followed by a continuation of the row between his chapel and the NGA over who should work the counter-stackers. Meanwhile, the transition from hot metal to 'cold type' was exceedingly slow. A date to typeset the *Times Literary Supplement* with the new equipment was fixed for February, and men were trained and ready to do it; but that date was missed and so was a second and a third. By midsummer the equipment was still lying idle.

These were only the most prominent issues. By May a drearily familiar pattern of lost copies of the *Sunday Times* had reasserted itself. The newspaper had failed to achieve its full print run on thirteen of the first nineteen issues of 1980, and only one issue, that of 3 February, had been distributed in full and on time. The company had lost £1,209,000 from this alone – £385,000 from copies that could not be sold because they were not printed, and the rest in cash that had to be paid in rebates to advertisers who had failed to reach all the readers they had paid for. One manager wrote plaintively to Mander: 'It is essential that the danger now be recognised for what it really is: a threat to the very future of the *Sunday Times*.'

The disruption revealed the real victor of the shutdown, which was not the company, the unions or the staff, but the fact of chapel power. That power had been partially hidden throughout the first half of the dispute by the issue of new technology, behind which the weight of an entire union, the NGA, had been mustered. Once that issue had been cleared out of the way, the chapels stood revealed as the dominating force. It was the chapels, first of Natsopa and then of the NGA, that dictated the pace of the protracted negotiations which led to the newspapers' return. Chapel power had not been overridden, either by the company or by the unions; so it had to be propitiated. And when the newspapers were back in print, the chapels continued to bestride the company's operations and to be the arbiters of production.

Could it have been different? Any judgement must start by recognising that the circumstances were unusual and perhaps unique. Times Newspapers was an inefficient company, whose Fleet Street rivals were just as inefficient, or even more so. Its technology was antiquated, but so was that of the other newspapers. It belonged to an industry whose nature – the production of national newspapers – protected it from international competition. It was not exposed to the same compulsion to change as steel or the motor industry, especially since it was further protected by the willingness of rich men and corporations to keep it going even when the newspapers did not make them the profits they ordinarily expected from their investments.

When the Times tried to strike out from the Fleet Street mould on its own, it came up against interest groups with strong incentives to resist. For in spite of its inefficiency, the existing state of things in Fleet Street provided many well-paid jobs. If the Times were successful, other newspapers would have to follow its example to stay competitive. In the long run a more efficient industry might provide more jobs. That was what had happened a century earlier when it had been revolutionised by mechanical methods – as now it was ready to be revolutionised by electronics. But such future benefits were speculative, and they would not necessarily fall to those who did best out of things as they were. The Times threatened the pattern of union influence and power as well as the pattern of production – and the pattern of rewards.

The unions not only had reasons to resist; they also had the means. The NGA and Slade could afford to keep their members idle almost indefinitely. Other unions, like Natsopa and Sogat, used their control over Fleet Street recruitment – and especially the casual labour system – to find their members other work during the shutdown, a form of outdoor relief in which they were hugely helped by the Times's rivals.

In this peculiar environment union power could not be defeated by the forces which the company deployed. If the unions could not achieve everything they wanted, they could certainly exercise a decisive veto against any management claim on them. Nor did union leaders have much influence. The casual system and the Fleet Street habit of constant bargaining had devolved all effective power into chapel hands. Only the chapels could make agreements, and nobody could compel them to do so – neither the company nor their own union leaders. The dispute might be going on even now if the company had not finally persuaded the chapels that it would close the newspapers for good unless they came to terms.

In retrospect, the company's strategy can be seen to have been full of flaws. Alarmed by disruptions in the first quarter of 1978, it responded by proposing myriad changes, small and large, then by setting a deadline for their acceptance. It could have eased the tensions by doing what the rest of Fleet Street had done; it could have broken the Government's pay policy and given its staff the wage increases their disruptions were aimed at winning. Instead, at the insistence of the Organisation, it chose the path of civic virtue, refused to pay and settled for a policy of either/or, on no better evidence that it would work than the ambiguous good will of union leaders whose influence with their Fleet Street members was manifestly slight.

Having chosen a strategy whose essence was persuasion, the company failed to persuade. Neither its promises nor its threats were forceful enough. It declared a crisis in April, but the staff heard little more than rumour until September. Thereafter management's eagerness to appear reasonable gave the impression of weakness. It did not lock out its members but gave them notice; a quarter of Times Newspapers' employees were not in danger of dismissal, and half were paid for more than three months after the newspapers were shut; the company postponed dismissals for two weeks after its November deadline; and it rehired staff in April with a promise that they would get all the pay they had lost. The company did not live up to the tough image it had cultivated.

Neither did the management succeed in persuading its staff to believe that its proposals contained real benefits. It communicated with its staff through union officials, and inevitably they put their own gloss on the company's plans. When at last the chapel members were given a sight of what the company intended for them, they found the advantages buried in paragraphs written in an unattractively peremptory style, which upset even the journalists. It took the ultimate threat of total closure to carry the staff – a year after persuasion might have been brought to bear. And when every normal conciliatory resource in the British industrial relations system had been tried, the company embarked on an unsuccessful adventure in Frankfurt.

There are points to be made in favour of the company's behaviour. By communicating through the unions, for instance, it showed that it was trying to play the negotiating game properly, by the book. And by giving the staff notice rather than locking them out, it tried to show a moderation that would earn a co-operative response. But however well-intentioned, the effect was an uneasy impression of tough talking mixed with weak action and an erratic, petulant aggressiveness. The company's presentation was fatal to the credibility that it had to establish if it were to succeed.

At times, too, managerial control seemed to slip disconcertingly between different levels of the Thomson Organisation. Questions like the importance of single keystroking, or whether journalists should be included among those to be sacked, or what penalties there should be for unofficial strikes were tossed back and forth between the Times board, the board of Thomson British Holdings in Stratford Place and the International Thomson Organisation across the Atlantic in Toronto. It made the direction of management policy uncertain, and it confused the staff.

In the front line of the dispute the Times board was itself divided. For instance, although at no time was there a split in the Times board or in the higher boards of the Thomson Organisation that was serious enough to lead to dissenting votes, there was continuing controversy about the right level at which to deal with the unions. Hussey and Nisbet-Smith consistently argued that the union leaders had to be involved. Dealing only with chapel fathers would inflate their standing, alienate the general secretaries and thus deprive the company of any chance of help from the union leadership. Other directors, like Hamilton and Harold Evans, leaned more towards dealing directly with the chapels. Such arguments were conducted in the privacy of the boardroom, but the divisions showed through. Directors were seen to act independently of one another. This was natural enough when each was responsible for a different part of an operation running normally, but it jarred badly when they were trying to manage a crisis between them, every nuance of which was being closely scrutinised by the unions and the staff.

A strange parallel with union attitudes was evident in the puritanism with which the Organisation conducted its side of the dispute. Both management and unions appeared to put abstractions and principles far above those material interests like jobs and money which are supposed to be the stuff of bargaining. The Organisation made Times Newspapers stick rigidly to the Government's pay policy, though no other newspaper in Fleet Street was doing so, and none suffered any penalty at the hands of the Government as a result. Yet it was this strict adherence to the pay limits that provoked the wave of unrest in the early months of 1978, and it was this unrest that led to the whole costly shutdown strategy. On the other side a similarly dogmatic rigidity prompted, among other things, the Natsopa clerical chapels' refusal to accept that there should be any redundancies among their members while at the same time agreeing to a lower number of clerical jobs. The chapels maintained their principle of rejecting redundancies in a way which only denied their members the chance to take redundancy money while reducing the number of actual jobs available and saving the company money. Paradoxically, if the Organisation had stuck to a balance-sheet view of its problems, it might have achieved more of its abstract aims, particularly the elusive right to manage. As it was, the long dispute only confirmed the power of the unions and, in many parts of the business, reduced managerial authority.

All this, of course, is written with the easy wisdom of hindsight. It fails to answer the question of what better alternative was open to the company. It could have followed the rest of Fleet Street and continued to muddle along in the familiar way. But that option would only have postponed the inevitable crisis of an industry which has for many years failed to face modern technical and economic realities. Unlike other newspapers, the Times at least posed the problems.

In the summer of 1980, a decent half-year after the newspapers were restarted, a discreet reshuffling of the top Times management took place. Hussey was made deputy chairman to Hamilton, charged among other things with travelling the world in search of new ideas. James Evans, who had started 25 years earlier fresh from university in the legal department of Kemsley Newspapers and risen under the Thomsons to become a director of Thomson British Holdings, returned to Gray's Inn Road to take over most of Hussey's functions as chief executive. Mike Mander left to run Thomson's magazine interests. Dugal Nisbet-Smith became managing director. There was no grand managerial purge, but the changes signalled a recognition that it was time for the old regime to give way.

The new regime examined the company's books – and shuddered at what it saw. Recession was beginning to bite heavily into revenues. The *Times*'s circulation had plunged back below 300,000. It was losing a great deal of money and so were its supplements. The *Sunday Times* would have been in profit if it had been able to produce all the copies it could sell; but it could not and as a result it, too, seemed destined to end the year in the red. Overall the company expected a pre-tax loss of £12 millions for the year. Technically it was insolvent and only massive loans from the parent Organisation let it continue, like a patient kept alive by constant transfusions of other people's blood.

Nor did the new regime find any comfort in the way things were going on the shop floor. When Nisbet-Smith met the FOCs of the production departments on 12 August he insisted on the over-riding importance of three points: an effective disputes procedure; the honouring of agreements to avoid production losses; and use of the new technology. But had we not heard these before? Were they not precisely the objectives the company had set itself more than two years earlier when it launched its 'big bang' strategy? And yet they seemed as distant as ever.

At the end of August industrial relations struck an as yet un-reached depth. *Times* journalists struck, for the first time in the newspaper's long history. They had taken a pay claim to an arbitrator, who recommended a rise of 21 per cent. The company, however, insisted that it could not pay more than the 18 per cent it had already offered. Though the arbitration was not binding on either side according to the chapel's agreement with the company, the journalists held that it should be, in honour if in nothing else. They, after all, had accepted a previous judgment from an arbitrator under the same procedure even though it had gone against them; why should the company not now accept the same disagreeable medicine? I have never met strikers more reluctant. But strike they did, in spite of their own profound misgivings and in spite of new threats from the management to close down the newspaper for good.

The Times was not the only newspaper company in the world to have fought fierce battles with its unions in the 1970s. Everywhere newspapers were faced with the same problems of rising costs and competition from other media, and everywhere solutions had been sought in staff reductions and new technology. As at the Times, managements had frequently been faced with powerful unions, for it is a fact of history that trade unions first appeared in most countries in the print trade, and print unions have become as firmly entrenched in many big-city newspapers elsewhere as they have in Fleet Street. The consequence was a long series of strikes and shutdowns, from Vancouver to Copenhagen.

But if the Times's problems were like those of other newspapers, the outcome of its battle was significantly different. Painful though the struggles elsewhere may have been, they generally led to a settlement. But at the Times little seemed to have been resolved. New technology was the most obvious case. In other countries ways of handling that had been settled even before the Times dispute began; but at the Times even the long shutdown failed to settle it. And the Times set the standard for the rest of Britain. Nowhere in the country would the NGA let newspaper people other than its own members operate the new keyboards, though it was by now commonplace to do so in most other countries.

If, allowing for all the special peculiarities of the Fleet Street environment, any lessons can be learned from the Times dispute about the condition of British industry in general, they are surely these: that the fragmented and competitive union set-up can make technical change extraordinarily hard to achieve, as the NGA's unwillingness to loosen its exclusive grip on the typesetting keyboards showed; and that the legal restraints on industrial action are so light that even the most thoroughly negotiated agreements can be discarded at will, as was shown by the continuing disruption of Times production.

The structure of union power was the only thing to emerge clearly enhanced from the Times shutdown. But could the dense tangle of conflicting union groups, each with its own claims to sovereign rights over links in the production chain and each with the ability to disrupt the newspapers, resolve the mass of problems that still confronted the Times and the rest of Fleet Street? Would union power be used to the advantage of union members and the newspapers? Would that power instead be a drag on both? Or would it even become, as it so often seemed in danger of doing, an end in itself, something to be manipulated for its own sake?

As the recession deepened in the second half of 1980, Fleet Street appeared ready to carry on as if it did not properly belong to the British economy. While industry was swept by waves of redundancies Fleet Street kept its belt-tightening to a minimum, as though nothing whatever was the matter. Typically, the *Observer* had to threaten total closure in order to persuade its machine managers' chapel to accept a wage packet for a single Saturday shift that was not far short of the average national wage for a full week's work.

But the *Observer*'s threat over the machine managers' claims was perhaps significant, as was the threat to close the *Times* when the journalists struck. Perhaps the new-style corporate managements had run out of patience and were no longer willing to tolerate the excesses of Fleet Street unions – excesses to which they had themselves given a new lease of life when the old-style proprietors had been unable any longer to bear them.

It may be that the shutdown of Times Newspapers was a painful episode in the regeneration of an industry – or in the industry's slow death. Both were possible. It would take time to tell which it was to be.

INDEX

Matthews, Victor, chairman, Express Group 109–10

May, Joe, director, Mirror Group 94

Metropole Hotel, Birmingham, meeting at (April 1978) 6–9, 12, 14

Miles, Bill, Sogat official 81

Mirchandani, Prakash, BBC TV reporter 86, 96, 136, 139, 144

Mirror Group Newspapers 37, 94

Moakes, John, Natsopa official 63

Montgomery, Field Marshal Bernard Law 10

Murray, Len, TUC gen. sec., 67, 68, 73, 74, 75–6, 117

Napoleon Bonaparte, Emperor 47

NAPs *see* New Agreement Proposals

National Board for Prices and Incomes 35

National Graphical Association (NGA) 8; background of 18–19; attempted merger with Slade 22; and new technology 22–4, 50–6, 68; and delay in negotiations 39–41, 44–5, 53–4; agrees to meet company 54; action by 66; fails to reach agreement 68, 70; financial strength of 71, 72, 152; and TUC 74, 76; and keystroking issue 74, 82–4, 118–22, 151, 157; and Booth's intervention 78, 80, 82–5; opposes Frankfurt edition 87, 92, 93, 94; journalists open dialogue with 93, 119–20; and deals with *Express* and *Observer* on new technology 112–13; agrees to set aside keystroking issue 121–2, 123; company proposals to 126–7; and delay in agreement 132–4, 151; final negotiations with 134–8, 140–3; and pay 134, 137–8, 147; machine managers of 142, 143; accepts arbitration 143–4; reaches agreement 144–5; conflict of with Natsopa 146, 151; and fining of supervisors 150–1; *and see* Dixon, Les

National Society of Operative Printers, Assistants and Media Personnel (Natsopa) 7, 19, 21–2, 27; and delay in negotiations 40;

Sunday Times chapels of 56–60 *and see* Brady, Reg; Fitzpatrick, Barry; and dismissal of *Sunday Times* clerks 60–2; begins negotiations 62–4, 65; Rirma branch of 64, 70, 116; action by 66; no agreement with 70; demands re-employment of staff 72–3; and keystroking issue 74, 84–5, 121–2; difficulty of negotiating with 116–17, 152, 155; slow negotiations with 128–34, 151; signs agreement (Oct. 1979) 134; pay offer to 137–8; conflict of with NGA 146, 151

National Union of Journalists (NUJ) 7, 19–20; decision by on international edition 92, 118; NGA talks with 119–20; and settlement 121, 122; *and see* Ashton, Ken

National Union of Printing, Bookbinding and Paper Workers 21

Natsopa *see* National Society of Operative Printers, Assistants and Media Personnel

New Agreement Proposals (NAPs) 44–5, 46–7, 62, 71

New Printing House Square: *Times* moved to 25; talks at (Nov. 1978) 54; (Oct. 1979) 135–7, 140–3

New York Times 95

Newspaper Publishers' Association (NPA) 4, 36–7, 57, 114

Newton, Gordon, editor, *Financial Times* 14

NGA *see* National Graphical Association

Nisbet-Smith, Dugal, gen. manager, Times Newspapers 33; at meeting with union leaders (April 1978) 7; background of 11–12; and delay in negotiations 41, 65, 66–7, 69, 70; and keystroking issue 54, 55, 74, 82–4; and Booth's intervention 78, 80; and change in strategy 115–17, 118, 120, 122; and proposals to union leaders 123; at Hamilton's meeting with FOCs 124–5, 126; goes to Blackpool 130–1; and final negotiations 134, 137, 141–3, 146; proposes arbitration 142–4; and fining of NGA supervisors 150;